The Sensible Sleep Solution

Wakefield Press

The Sensible Sleep Solution

A guide to sleep in your baby's first year

Sarah Blunden and Angie Willcocks

Wakefield Press
16 Rose Street
Mile End
South Australia 5031
www.wakefieldpress.com.au

First published 2012
Reprinted 2016, 2018, 2020

Copyright © Sarah Blunden and Angie Willcocks, 2012

All rights reserved. This book is copyright. Apart from any fair dealing for the purposes of private study, research, criticism or review, as permitted under the Copyright Act, no part may be reproduced without written permission. Enquiries should be addressed to the publisher.

Edited by Julia Beaven, Wakefield Press
Designed by Mark Thomas
Images on pages 5, 47, 71, 81, 88, 96, 132
    copyright © istockphoto
Images on pages 44, 61, 68, 114, 122, 142, 150
    copyright © Shutterstock

National Library of Australia Cataloguing-in-Publication entry

Author: Blunden, Sarah.
Title: The sensible sleep solution: a guide to sleep in your baby's first year / Sarah Blunden and Angie Willcocks.
ISBN: 978 1 86254 947 0 (paperback).
Notes: Includes bibliographical references and index.
Subjects: Infants – Sleep.
Other Authors/Contributors: Willcocks, Angie.
Dewey Number: 649.122

This publication contains the opinions and ideas of its authors. Although differing opinions abound regarding the information contained in this book, all the information herein is based on recent research and is therefore evidence based. All efforts were made to ensure the accuracy of the information contained in this publication as of the date of writing. It is sold on the understanding that the authors and publisher are not engaged in rendering professional advice or services in the publication. If the reader or user of the publication requires personal advice or services a competent health professional should be sought.

The authors and publisher specifically disclaim any responsibility for any liability, or risk, personal or otherwise, which is incurred, as a consequence, directly or indirectly, of the use or application of the contents of this book. This book is not intended to provide a complete and exhaustive treatment of the subject; nor is it a substitute for advice from your medical practitioner, who knows your circumstances best. Seek medical attention promptly for any specific medical condition or problem that your child may have. Furthermore, it is an understanding that all products discussed in this book should comply with Australian national safety standards.

Dr Sarah Blunden and Angie Willcocks

Contents

Introduction ... 1

Part One ... 5

Everything you need to know about your baby's sleep

- Definitions of active and quiet sleep ... 6
- Circadian rhythms and the development of night sleep ... 7
- Why a baby wakes ... 8
- Sleep associations ... 9
- Where will my baby sleep? ... 17
- SIDS and safety ... 21
- Temperament and sleep ... 25
- The crying baby ... 34

Part Two ... 47

The Sensible Sleep Solution

- What is it? ... 48
- Self-soothing ... 49
- The Sensible Sleep Solution and controlled crying ... 50
- Attachment ... 53
- Brain development ... 58
- Learning, controlled crying and the Sensible Sleep Solution ... 65
- Routines and rituals ... 66

Part Three   71

Taking care of yourself

- Coping with less sleep   72
- Diet   72
- Exercise   73
- Rest and relaxation   73
- Housework   75
- Partnership/Relationship   76
- Balancing your baby's needs with your own   76
- How are you going?   77

Part Four   81

Age groups and routines

- Birth to Four Weeks   82
- Four to Eight Weeks   92
- Eight to Twelve Weeks   98
- Twelve to Sixteen Weeks   105
- Four to Six Months   115
- Six to Eight Months   124
- Eight to Ten Months   133
- Ten to Twelve Months   144

Conclusion   155
Glossary   156
Resources   160
References   162
Index   164

Acknowledgements

This book has been a long time in the making and there are many people to thank.

Thank you to all the parents who have contributed case studies and insights, some names have been changed as requested.

Thanks to our friends and families who have proofread and formatted the manuscript at various points, and who have been positive and encouraging along the way.

Special thanks to Dr Ramona Chryssidis, general practitioner, for her helpful insights and advice on the gastro-oesophageal reflux section.

Many thanks to Julia Beaven from Wakefield Press for her patient and supportive editing.

And of course many, many thanks to our families, Philippe and Kelly, Gary, Matilda and Hazel for being supportive, encouraging and (most of the time!) patient over the writing and editing of *The Sensible Sleep Solution*.

Introduction

Did you know that by 12 months of age 15 to 30 per cent of babies are likely to have a sleep problem? The good news is that most sleep problems in toddlers are preventable, and this book tells you how.

Unlike other books on baby sleep, this book is based on a middle road of baby sleep advice that lies somewhere between the extremes of giving in (i.e. having your baby share your bed when you'd prefer not to) or leaving your baby cry for increasing periods (controlled crying). The information in this book is based on the latest evidence and research around infant sleep. Look for a number at the end of a sentence to indicate the source of the information; all books and research papers referred to are listed at the back of this book.

There is no shortage of advice about baby sleep. Some people will tell you that you can quickly get your baby into a routine and back to normal life without too much fuss; others will tell you that your life (and sleep) will never be the same again. Some 'experts' will try to convince you of the need to teach your baby to sleep; others will tell you that letting your baby cry will result in long-term psychological damage. With a lot of information available and with so much supposedly hanging in the balance, it is no wonder that many new parents feel anxious about their baby's sleep and what to do about it. This book is a realistic and sensible guide to your baby's development and how this relates to sleep, and provides practical information and tips for the first year.

In reality the first year of a baby's life is a time of great adjustment and it is important that you know that your sleep will, without a doubt, be affected by the arrival of your baby. This is inevitable even with the best-behaved baby in the world. The good news is that there are steps you can take to minimise the likelihood of normal sleep disruptions becoming sleep problems. To do this, it is important to be aware of the facts on infant development, how this may affect sleep, and what you can do to help your baby develop healthy self-soothing and sleep habits at different stages throughout their first year.

The aim of this book is to outline a road map of what your baby's sleep patterns will probably be like in the first 12 months, and provide some tips on how to head in the direction of a happy and well-rested family.

This book is for parents who:
+ want to know *factual* information, based on evidence from research on the how and why of baby sleep
+ want to have the knowledge and understanding about their baby's sleep so they can make their *own* decisions about how they settle their child, based not on hearsay nor value judgments, but on facts and research in simple language
+ don't want to leave their baby to cry in distress
+ want to understand where their baby is at developmentally over the first year and the importance of *self-soothing* for baby's sleep
+ would like their baby to be sleeping well in their own bed, in their own room (or in a room with a sibling) by the age of 12 months.

We encourage you to see this as a map or a journey outline rather than a quick-fix book. It is important to have realistic expectations and goals. While it is not necessarily realistic or fair to expect your baby to fit in with you and your life in the first few months, it is reasonable to expect that you and your baby will be fitting in with each other by the end of the first year.

This book has four parts. **Part 1** provides information about sleep (where your baby might sleep, characteristics of baby sleep), about how babies differ, crying and keeping your baby safe when sleeping. **Part 2** explains in detail our method – the Sensible Sleep Solution; how and why it helps your baby develop good sleep patterns over the first year, and how it differs from other methods. You will find information about taking care of yourself in your baby's first year in **Part 3**. We have included this important section to highlight that parents' wellbeing is imperative for children's wellbeing; put another way: you can't look after your baby if you don't look after yourself. In **Part 4** we discuss realistic expectations for sleep in relation to development for specific age groups, provide sleep tips and practical help.

A series of icons throughout the book will alert you to interesting information and advice on particular topics. There are four icons:

 Of interest: Information relevant to sleep and settling that we think you'll find interesting.

 Our thoughts: Our ideas, thoughts and advice on particular topics.

 In a nutshell: A summary or important snippet from the information discussed.

 Tips: Practical tips and advice for frequently encountered problems or concerns.

It is our hope that this book, which introduces you to the Sensible Sleep Solution, will help you feel more knowledgeable and in control in your first year as a parent, reassure you and, most importantly, allow you to enjoy your time with your new baby without the stress of sleep issues!

Part One

Everything you need to know about your baby's sleep

Most people realise that there are different types of being awake, such as actively thinking, relaxing and exercising. Not everyone realises that there are also different types of being asleep. When we sleep we go though different stages of sleep. In adults two of these stages are 'rapid eye movement sleep' (REM) and 'non-rapid eye movement sleep' (NREM). In babies the different types of sleep are called 'active' and 'quiet' sleep, and at birth babies spend equal time in these types of sleep. At about eight months of age, as the human brain develops, active sleep becomes rapid eye movement sleep (REM) and quiet sleep becomes non-rapid eye movement sleep (NREM).

Sleep is a natural state that babies will acquire on their own when the conditions are right. Staying asleep happens when babies learn to soothe themselves to sleep.

Definitions of active and quiet sleep

Active sleep, like the REM sleep it will become, is very light sleep. If you are watching your baby during active sleep you will see her squirm, jerk, grimace and move around. She is sleeping lightly, and at the end of the active stage she will wake slightly. Adults and older children also rouse slightly, but when babies do they are often unable to get back to sleep without help, and they may cry or fuss.

Young babies spend a lot of time in the active sleep stage; much more than older children and adults spend in REM. Active sleep is light sleep so babies wake often during this stage, and it is also normal to wake after a cycle of active sleep. Another reason why they wake is because babies have tiny tummies and need to be fed small amounts often. Waking is actually a normal part of the sleep process. What your baby needs to learn throughout their first year is getting back to sleep.[3]

Quiet sleep, as the name suggests, is a quieter and calmer sleep. During this phase your baby will be sleeping peacefully, not jerking or moving around as much as in the active sleep phase. Quiet sleep develops over the first year into non-rapid eye movement sleep and eventually differentiates further into four stages of quiet sleep known as stages 1, 2, 3, and 4. Of these, stage 4 is the deepest sleep.[3]

Circadian rhythms and the development of night sleep

Sleep is regulated by many bodily systems. One of the most important is the circadian system. This system helps us fall asleep when we are tired and plays an important role in the pattern of sleeping and waking.

The development of the circadian system is influenced in part by light (day) and dark (night), by cultural and social factors and, most significantly, by brain development. At birth, the circadian system is not fully functional. What this means is that it is not possible for a newborn's brain to register that it is day or night, or to understand that night-time is the right time to have the longest stretch of sleep.

Research shows that the 24-hour circadian system does not start to develop until ten or 11 weeks after birth.[2] The good news is that there are things that can be done to encourage and support the development of the circadian system; that is, to help your baby learn that night-time is the time that we humans like to have our longest sleep! Once your baby's circadian rhythm is well developed her longest sleep will naturally occur during the night, and you will find it much easier to establish a routine.

So what can you do to encourage the development of the circadian rhythm?

Allow your baby some time outside in the bright light when she is awake.[4] (Remembering to protect her from direct sunlight, of course.)

Start to establish a routine by putting your baby to bed at about the same time every night and getting up at the same time each morning. As we will see later in this book, some babies are easier to guide into a routine than others, but focusing on the circadian rhythm is a good place to start.

Why a baby wakes

It is natural and normal for babies to wake regularly from sleep. Adults wake as well, but are normally unaware of this because, over time, we have learnt to settle easily and readily to sleep. Babies wake more because they spend more time in light sleep and because their tiny tummies require frequent feeding. Many babies do not know how to get back to sleep, and this skill needs to be learnt.

There are many reasons why a baby may wake from sleep. These include:

+ a natural wake after a REM or active-sleep stage
+ hunger
+ wind
+ an uncomfortably wet or dirty nappy
+ a need for comfort and closeness
+ something external (such as noise or temperature)
+ pain or discomfort (from teething, an illness or a medical condition).[5]

 A sleep-disturbed baby is defined as 'one who is unable to settle back to sleep without the parents being aware of the wakening'.[1]

Sleep associations

A sleep association is a behaviour that comes, over time and regular use, to be associated with the process of falling asleep. Adults and children may have sleep associations, using, for example, the television, a particular pillow, thumb sucking, hair twirling or even the presence of a partner in the bed to help them fall asleep. However, if those sleep associations are missing, falling asleep can become difficult.

In babies a sleep association often develops around something that the parent introduces to aid sleep, such as wrapping, a dummy, or a lullaby toy. Other sleep associations that commonly develop in infancy are rocking, patting, breastfeeding and the presence of a parent in bed with the baby. These sleep associations become problematic if they are used so frequently and consistently that the baby becomes *reliant* on the association to fall asleep, and *unable* to fall asleep without it. Let's say, for example, that you consistently rock your baby to sleep. Over time, rocking will become a sleep association for your baby; he will grow reliant on rocking to fall asleep, and will cry whenever he wakes slightly because he won't be able to get back to sleep until he is rocked again.

our thoughts

It is important to note that even when parents have the best of intentions babies frequently do develop sleep associations that are not ideal in the long term. Some habits, which suit everybody in the beginning (such as breastfeeding to sleep or wrapping), may turn out, a few months later, to be less than ideal for parents. If this happens it is not the end of the world, there are many opportunities to undo unwanted sleep associations over the first year. It is important to realise though, it is unlikely that removing a sleep association will be stress free – or cry free. Try to avoid parent-dependent sleep associations.

Many parents offer their babies a sleep aid in an attempt to help them fall asleep initially, and then to settle again after waking. If the sleep aid provides comfort in the absence of the parent – encouraging self-soothing – they can become an effective sleep association. Examples of sleep aids that may be comforting in a parent's absence are a soft toy or a lullaby toy and, eventually, a dummy (see Sleep Associations Table 1, p. 2).

You can introduce a soft and soothing toy to your baby's bedtime routine before six months of age. The object will – over time – come to be associated with feelings of calm and relaxation, and will eventually become comforting to the baby in your absence. However, it is not recommended that infants under 12 months of age take any toy to bed with them because of the risk of suffocation.

Should sleep associations be avoided?

Not all sleep associations should be avoided, just those that rely on a parent's input. To minimise the likelihood that your baby will develop a sleep association that requires your presence, two things are important:

+ Use a range of settling techniques, avoiding reliance on one settling technique to the exclusion of others.
+ Allow your baby to calm down and grow sleepy and relaxed with whatever settling/calming technique works best, and then change the technique or leave the baby to see if they can continue to fall asleep without help. For example, calm your baby with rocking or patting, and then when the baby is calm and drowsy, stop the rocking or patting, and sit still or place the baby in their bed.

Sometimes babies develop their own sleep habits and associations quite independent from the ones their parents offer them. Such habits may be hair twirling or thumb, finger or hand sucking. The types of sleep associations that babies use and prefer may change as they grow older due to individual preferences and what is available or offered to them. For example, a four-month-old who is wrapped with both hands tucked in will be unable to use her thumbs, fingers, or hands to suck on and so may come to prefer her dummy and lullaby toy as her soothing object. Older babies may prefer a soft toy or piece of material as their soothing sleep object.

Tips for choosing a soothing sleep toy for your baby

COMFORT TOYS

Choose something that is machine washable, with no loose buttons, clips or attachments that may fall (or be sucked or chewed) off. Make sure there is no string or ribbon of any sort that may entangle little fingers. Any toys that can cover a baby's face during sleep are not recommended.

Size is important – you want something not too big for carrying around or travelling with, but not too small that it may easily become lost or misplaced in your baby's bed.

LULLABY TOYS

Choose something that your baby can learn to operate themselves at some point (but be realistic, this may not happen until the end of the first year). If the toy has a light of some sort, ensure that the light is orange because orange light will not stimulate your baby to keep it awake. Bear in mind that you will also have to listen to this toy many times, so choose a tune you find pleasant!

Table 1: Sleep associations.

SLEEP AID	PROS	CONS	AVOID THE PROBLEM	OTHER ISSUES
Dummies	Babies love to suck. Babies like dummies for self-soothing. After the first month, dummies are more effective for calming a baby than rocking.[6] Babies who use dummies have lighter sleep and lighter sleep is protective against SIDS. Some studies have shown that the use of a dummy is protective against SIDS.[7]	The Australian Breastfeeding Association recommends that dummies should not be given to breastfed babies under 1 month of age. Babies can come to rely on the dummy for soothing. If they do, there will be times when the baby cannot replace the dummy and parents will need to. Breathing through the nose is difficult if a baby has a cold, so baby will need to spit out the dummy to breathe. Parents will need to repeatedly replace the dummy.	Try using the dummy to get your baby to a sleepy state, and then remove it when your baby is drowsy but not asleep. Only allow the dummy to be used at certain times (such as when calming your baby at bedtime, when your baby is unwell, in the car). From about 8–10 months of age you can start teaching your baby to pick up the dummy and put it in their mouth. Let your baby practise with a few dummies scattered around them. The cherry-shaped dummies are cheap to buy and may be easier for your baby to put in themselves. Use a nasal saline solution or nasal aspirator to clear your baby's congested nose (see your doctor or pharmacist for more information).	Never use a ribbon to attach the dummy to your baby. Frequently check the dummy to make sure that it is intact, clean and not in need of replacement. Ensure that the dummy you have chosen meets safety standards. If you are going to offer your baby a dummy consider the challenge of taking that dummy away before your baby/toddler is ready to give it up (sometime in the preschool years or possibly later). Do not dip the dummy in sweet foods like honey to encourage sucking. This practice is likely to cause dental caries.

Table 1 continued: Sleep associations.

SLEEP AID	PROS	CONS	AVOID THE PROBLEM	OTHER ISSUES
Thumb sucking	Babies love to suck. Babies can have access to their thumb whenever they want to calm themselves, and parent help is not needed.	Parents can control the use of a dummy for soothing but they can't control the use of the baby's thumb.	Replace with a dummy that you can control more readily. Encourage the use of other soothing strategies, such as reliance on a comfort toy.	A baby may suck their fingers when dirty and this may worry some parents. Teeth alignment might be affected by thumb sucking.
Wrapping (swaddling)	Wrapping a baby snugly may help them settle and stay settled by minimising the jerking caused by a startle reflex (see Moro reflex p. 83).	Babies can come to rely on the feeling of being very snug (and the wrapping that causes the feeling) to get to sleep. From about 4 months of age your baby may wriggle out of their wrap and need re-wrapping to settle. In hot weather wrapping may not be appropriate.	Half-wrap (wrap with one arm out) for some (e.g. day) or all sleeps. This can be started from birth, or around 2–3 months of age. Only wrap at night. Get a wrap that is designed to stay put around the baby. When you want to wean your baby from wrapping, use a lightweight sleeping bag (so their hands can get free) then firmly tuck a sheet over this.	Wrapping a baby can cause overheating. To ensure this does not happen dress your baby lightly (see temperature p. 22), wrap only in cotton, and keep the room between 16 and 20°C. It is not generally considered safe to wrap a baby's arms once they roll as they may roll onto their tummy and not be able to roll back. Wrapping is not recommended if you are co-sleeping (see SIDS information p. 23). Make sure that the wrap you choose will not pose the risk of covering your baby's face or entanglement.

Table 1 continued: Sleep associations.

SLEEP AID	PROS	CONS	AVOID THE PROBLEM	OTHER ISSUES
Soft toys	Can support self-soothing by helping your baby to feel comforted by a familiar object at sleep time (see transitional objects p. 121).	Baby may become dependent on one toy for comfort and the toy may become lost either in the bed at night-time and parents may be called to help find it, or during the day when out.	Buy two of the same/similar toys in case one is lost or misplaced. Only provide the toy for relaxing or bedtimes (and ensure it is not to be taken outside) to minimise the likelihood of losing it and to preserve its role as a sleep comfort toy. From 12 months of age, teach your baby how to look for and find the toy in their bed (a dim nightlight may help with this).	It is not recommended that soft toys are in the cot with babies under 12 months of age due to suffocation risk. Comfort toys should be machine washable for hygiene purposes and have no attachments that may come loose (such as ribbons, buttons or clips) as these may pose choking and/or suffocation risk.
Lullaby toys with music	Can be a very useful addition to the bedtime routine, providing baby with a stimulus that is familiar, comforting and calming to the senses.	Many toys require parental assistance to start (all for most of the first year).	Choose a toy that your baby can learn to operate over time. Choose a toy you can take travelling with you (not too big or bulky).	Some lullaby toys are not recommended for babies younger than 6 months of age due to risk of suffocation. Check the product information. Lullaby toys that attach to the side of the cot are usually suitable from birth as they are not in the cot with the baby.

Table 1 continued: Sleep associations.

SLEEP AID	PROS	CONS	AVOID THE PROBLEM	OTHER ISSUES
Music or white noise (background noise such as a fan or a radio off station)	Some babies are soothed by constant noise. Can mask other household noises.	Baby may become dependent on that sound to get to sleep, particularly if the music is left on while baby is falling asleep.	Avoid leaving the music on every time baby goes to sleep. Use the music as part of the 'wind-down' process but turn it off when baby is drowsy but awake. Use a portable CD player when travelling.	At low volume there are no safety concerns.

Case study

I thought I would never give my child a dummy. My partner was happy to give Luka one as soon as we left the maternity ward. So we discussed giving him a dummy and decided that once I was confident with my breastfeeding we would give a dummy a try if we needed to.

The first night we gave him a dummy, at about four weeks, it was because he was so unsettled and I didn't know what else to do. The biggest difference with a dummy is his night sleep. In the past he would wake up unsettled and no matter what I tried I would need to pick him up. Now he often wakes and sucks on his dummy and resettles himself.

I'm glad I waited a bit to give it to him though, because I think I know him better now and I'm not worried about whether he needs a feed or not.

Joanne, mother of Luka, eight weeks

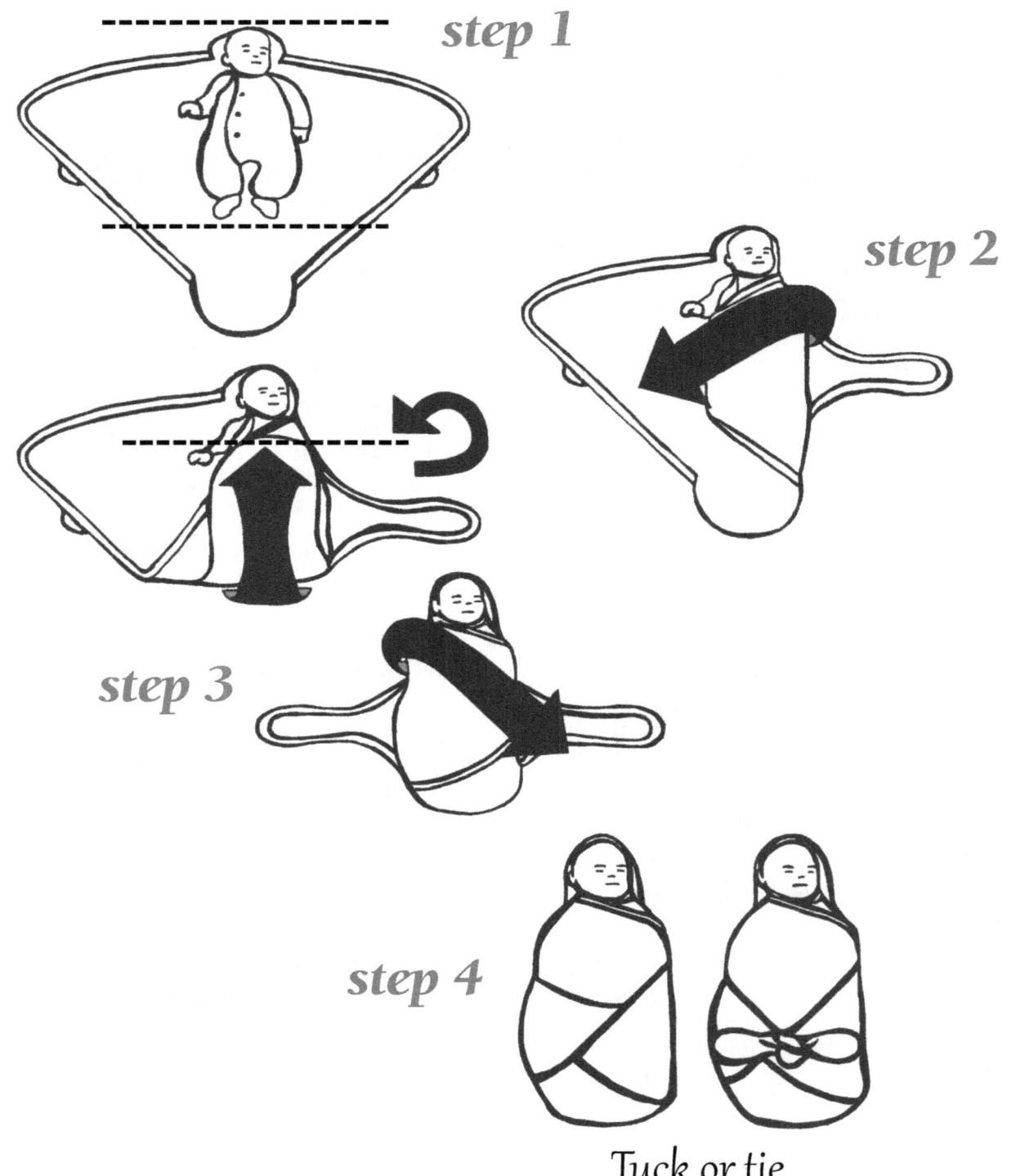

How to swaddle or wrap

Step 1: Spread blanket and place your baby in the middle, up high, with his neck touching the top edge.

Step 2: Pull the left side of the blanket snugly in a diagonal direction across your baby's body. Make sure his right arm is wrapped close to his body. Securely tuck the blanket under his bottom.

Step 3: Bring the bottom of the blanket up and fold the edge over as much as needed to adjust for size (as your baby grows, you will be folding over less). Then pull the right corner of the blanket across your baby's body, securing his left arm near his body, and tuck the blanket under his bottom.

Step 4: There will be two remaining flaps. For a secure bundle, tuck the flaps under your baby's back between the two fabrics.

Where will my baby sleep?
You have the following options:
- in their own cot/bassinet/bed
    - in their own room
    - in your room
    - in a sibling's room
- in bed with one parent
- in bed with both parents.

our thoughts

Wherever you decide your baby will sleep, it is important to think about creating a comfortable and practical area for night feeding and changing.

In an area of low light you may want to set up a comfortable feeding chair and a change station with everything you might need, including:
+ a drink for yourself
+ nappies and wipes
+ a cloth for wiping up any mess
+ a complete change of clothes for your baby (just in case!)
+ a heater or extra blanket for yourself and your baby in the cooler months.

Table 2: Where should my baby sleep?

SLEEPING PLACE	PROS	CONS
In own bed in own room	The normal noises of baby sleep will be less likely to disturb your sleep. Baby will have the opportunity to associate their own bed with sleeping alone, and will develop self-soothing strategies in this environment. Less impact on parents' sex life. Some researchers think that it may be important for children to have their own bed, to help them develop healthy sleep habits.	Some parents feel less confident or secure with the baby in another room, and so feel that their sleep is more affected because of anxiety about the baby's wellbeing. In the early months a baby is more likely to fully wake to alert parents for a feed (and therefore may be more difficult to settle after the feed). It's more difficult to be aware of and monitor baby's environment (such as temperature) if they are in another room. A baby monitor may be needed if the room is a distance from the parents' room, or the parents are heavy sleepers.
In own bed in parents' room	In the early months a baby may not fully wake when needing a feed, thus making her easier to settle. Endorsed by the SIDS Council[7] as a safe option. There is a decreased risk of SIDS when an infant sleeps in the same room as the parents (but not in the same bed). Parents may feel more secure knowing their baby is close by. Parents can more easily monitor their baby's environment e.g. room temperature.	Parents sleep may be disrupted if they are acutely aware of every noise the baby makes. After the first few months a baby may be disturbed by the parents in the room. Parents should agree to room sharing with their baby or their relationship may suffer.
In own bed in sibling's room	Room sharing may support close sibling relationships.	The children may disrupt each other with different bed times and/or night waking.

Table 2 continued: Where should my baby sleep?

SLEEPING PLACE	PROS	CONS
Bed sharing with parent(s)	Parent/s may feel a close connection to their child and may believe that this connection is not possible if not bed sharing (this is not backed up by research). Breastfeeding at night is likely to be less disruptive, and may encourage breastfeeding to continue for longer. Some parents say that they get more sleep in a bed-sharing arrangement.	Bed sharing is not recommended by the SIDS Council of Australia, due to the increased risk of SIDS and sleep accidents.[9] A baby may not have adequate opportunity to develop self-soothing, as the parent is present during the night. A baby is very likely to come to rely on parental assistance to get back to sleep. Some parents can grow to resent having no space away from their baby, impacting on daytime parenting. Weaning from the breast may be more difficult. The parents' relationship may be detrimentally affected (including re-establishing a sexual relationship) if both parents do not agree with the decision. Bed sharing is not a safe option if either parent smokes, has consumed alcohol or drugs or has pillows or bedding (see p. 23 for more information on bedding).

What else about sleeping arrangements?

If you both make the decision to share a bed with your baby (rather than if it just happens), there is a better chance of it working for you and not causing bad feeling.

It is not *necessary* for you and your baby to sleep together for your baby to feel happy and relaxed and attached to you. For more information on the factors involved in healthy attachment see p. 53 in Part 2.

Advocates for co-sleeping often make the point that primates share a sleeping space, and that this happens in many other cultures as well. Does this mean that they always produce healthy and happy offspring because they sleep together?

Having your baby sleep in your bed occasionally will not necessarily lead to her having trouble sleeping alone later but it is important to remember that even occasional co-sleeping must follow safe sleeping guidelines (see p. 23). If you find you are taking your baby into your own bed more than you would like to, but it seems to be the only way you can get any sleep, don't despair, you can reduce the likelihood of this becoming a problem by:

+ *always* settling your baby in their bed at the beginning of the night and for day sleeps
+ ensuring that there is distance between your baby and you as you sleep (so that your baby does not get used to snuggling up to you for comfort all night, thus waking as soon as contact is broken). Maintaining a distance is also important for safe sleeping
+ using a small bassinet-type device that can fit in your bed. This will allow many of the benefits of co-sleeping while minimising the risks
+ getting up as soon as your baby is settled (as hard as it is when you are so tired!) and putting her back in her cot or bassinet
+ using a soothing sleep object such as a cuddle toy to help comfort and settle your baby while she is in bed with you. Over time, your baby will come to associate this object with good feelings of being calm and comfortable. Eventually the object itself will help her self-soothe on its own. Remember, this toy should not be a soft toy that can cover her face.

Did you know? The ideal room temperature for sleeping is between 16 and 22°C. What your baby wears to bed depends on whether you are wrapping or using a sleeping bag. A general rule of thumb is that a baby will need one more layer than an adult would in the same room. A baby who is wrapped is likely to need one less layer than a baby who is not wrapped.

SIDS and safety

Sudden Infant Death Syndrome (SIDS) is the sudden and unexplained death of a child under one year of age. SIDS is listed as a cause of death in cases where an infant dies suddenly and unpredictably (usually during sleep) and no cause can be found even after a thorough medical investigation. The peak risk period for SIDS is between two and four months.

Sleeping accidents are accidents that happen while the baby is sleeping or while they are in their sleeping space. Sleeping accidents may cause injury or death but are not the same as SIDS. SIDS is not listed as the cause of death in situations where the cause of an infant's death is known, even if they die during sleep. Examples of sleeping accidents are suffocation, strangulation or entrapment (e.g. down the side of a couch).

The cause of SIDS is not known and no cure has been found. However, the introduction of Reducing the Risks of SIDS program in Australia in the early 1990s has dramatically reduced the number of SIDS deaths.

Reducing the risks of SIDS
(NATIONAL SIDS COUNCIL OF AUSTRALIA)

Put your baby to sleep on their back. The risk of SIDS is increased if babies sleep on their stomachs, and some studies have shown an increased risk in babies who are put on their side to sleep.

Make sure your baby's head remains uncovered during sleep. If your baby's head becomes covered (for example by a quilt, blanket, pillow or soft toy) this increases the risk of SIDS. It is best to wrap your baby securely with sheets firmly tucked in (see diagram on p. 16) or use a zip-up sleeping bag that your baby cannot slip down into. Babies should not have quilts, cot bumpers or soft toys in bed with them in the first year.

Keep your baby's environment smoke free. The risk of SIDS is increased if the mother smokes. If both parents smoke then the risk of SIDS is doubled.

Other SIDS considerations

1. The baby's temperature

There is an increased risk of SIDS if the infant becomes too hot or too cold. It is important to try to maintain a comfortable temperature in whichever room a baby is sleeping, and the ideal is between 16 and 22°C. (Remember that smoke alarms should be installed in any room that has a heater in it, *especially* if people sleep in that room.)

It can seem very difficult to know if your baby is too hot or too cold. Test your baby's warmth by feeling his tummy and/or cheeks, not his hands.

+ A flushed face that feels hot to the touch is a sign that your baby is too hot. Also check if he is damp from perspiration on his scalp and/or behind his neck. Some babies cry if they are too hot, but others don't. Other babies become lethargic if they are too hot.
+ Check to see if your baby's cheeks or tummy are cold to the touch. Frequent waking through the night in the cooler months (when there are no other concerns) may be an indication that he is too cold. Some babies may cry if they are too cold, others will not.

2. Co-sleeping (sharing a bed with your baby)
Co-sleeping with your baby does not protect her from SIDS. In fact, studies show there is an increased risk of an infant dying from SIDS when mothers who smoke, or smoked during pregnancy, co-sleep with their babies.

Co-sleeping may also increase the risk of *sleep accidents* for your baby. Sleep accidents include suffocation from bedding, being rolled on, falling out of bed or becoming trapped between the bed and the wall. If you choose to co-sleep with your baby, even for just some of the time, it is very important that you minimise the risks associated with co-sleeping.

Recommendations for safer co-sleeping:
+ No co-sleeping if either you or your partner has been using drugs (prescription or recreational) or has been drinking alcohol.
+ Consider whether you and/or your partner are very heavy sleepers and difficult to rouse; if so, co-sleeping may not be a safe option for your family.
+ The only bedding that should be used for the first six months is a well-secured fitted sheet. This means no top sheets, blankets, quilts or pillows of any sort. You will need to wear appropriate clothes to bed that will keep you warm without the need for bedding.
+ Ensure that the mattress is firm, flat and smooth, with no dips that your baby may roll into.
+ Do not co-sleep if you have a waterbed.

+ Make sure your baby can't fall out of the bed or become trapped in between the bed and wall, or the bed and bedhead, or any other piece of furniture. Be aware that some guard rails for the sides of the bed (designed for toddlers moving into a big bed) are not recommended for use with infants, and may pose an entrapment risk. Elizabeth Pantley,[8] author of *The No Cry Sleep Solution,* has co-slept with all four of her children and suggests that the best way to avoid the risk of entrapment and falling is to put the mattress on the floor for you all to sleep on.
+ You may want to invest in a bassinet that fits in your bed for the times that your baby shares your bed. Such devices may allow many of the benefits of co-sleeping while reducing the risk.

3. Breastfeeding
While some studies show that breastfeeding decreases the risk of SIDS, others don't.

4. Immunisations
There is no evidence that immunisation is associated with an increased risk of SIDS.

5. Dummies/pacifiers
Some studies have shown that the use of a dummy is protective against SIDS.[9]

6. Mattress cover
Some research has suggested that the bacteria, moulds and other allergens on and in mattresses play a role in SIDS.[29] Not all researchers agree but it does make sense to use a well-fitted washable mattress cover (and wash it regularly). Some researchers suggest a new mattress should be used for each baby.

7. Side sleeping

Some babies with gastro-oesphageal reflux may sleep better on their left side.[10] However some studies show an increased risk of SIDS for infants placed on their sides compared to on their backs.[7, 10, 11] This may be because babies roll from their side onto their tummy, which is a risk factor for SIDS. If you choose to place your baby on his side to sleep, you can help ensure his safety by ensuring:

+ he is not wrapped
+ his lower arm is well forward to stop him rolling onto his tummy.

Temperament and sleep

Temperament refers to the personal characteristics that people are born with. Temperament is largely genetically determined, but is also influenced by experiences in-utero. Temperament and life experience (from in-utero as well as after the birth) come together over time to eventually make up what is known as 'personality'. Personality is influenced by two parts of the brain, the limbic system, and the frontal lobe (see p. 61). The frontal lobe continues developing for a long time after birth, and how it develops is influenced greatly by what people experience. The limbic system, however, is more or less fully developed at birth and is responsible for whether or not people are *temperamentally* likely to react in a positive or negative way to new experiences.

In a nutshell

Babies are born with their own unique characteristics, these characteristics are then affected by what happens in a baby's life and both of these factors make up what we call personality.

What does this mean for sleep?

Is it true that some babies are simply better sleepers than others? Yes. Some babies are adept at calming themselves from birth, while others take longer to learn this skill, and need more support to achieve it. Some babies have more difficulty getting to sleep and staying asleep than others, and some babies' sleep is more readily disrupted by changes than others. All of these differences are in large part because of differences in temperament. Research has shown that babies differ, from birth, in how their bodies react to new experiences and stress.[12]

Below is a table on the characteristics of temperament, how these characteristics may affect your baby's sleep, and some ideas on how you can support the development of healthy sleep habits with consideration of your baby's temperament.[13]

Table 3: Temperament and its effect on your baby's sleep.

TEMPERAMENT CHARACTERISTIC	WHAT IT REFERS TO	HOW IT MIGHT AFFECT SLEEP	HOW PARENTS CAN HELP
Activity level	How physically active/energetic infant is.	Less placid, more active babies might need more help to transition from active time to sleep time. It may be more difficult to recognise tired signs in a very active baby. Active babies may seem to have less need for sleep and may be more active when he is sleeping e.g. jerking and moving.	Allow your baby to have active awake times. Important to have a wind-down time that does not involve physical activity. Start the wind-down time when you think your baby might be or should be getting tired rather than waiting until tired signs are obvious, by then your baby may be overtired. Try wrapping to calm your baby.

Table 3 continued: Temperament and its effect on your baby's sleep.

TEMPERAMENT CHARACTERISTIC	WHAT IT REFERS TO	HOW IT MIGHT AFFECT SLEEP	HOW PARENTS CAN HELP
Rhythmicity (also called regularity)	This refers to biological regularity – how regular is baby's sleep/wake cycle, eating patterns and digestive processes (i.e. pooing).	If your baby is more regular and rhythmical in his biological functions he will be easier to read and predict. Establishing a routine will be easier with your baby if he is more regular and rhythmical.	Recognise that if your baby is not very regular/rhythmical then it may take longer to develop a routine. Be reassured that regularity will emerge as your baby matures.
Approach or withdrawal	How positively a baby reacts to new people, places and things.	A baby who doesn't seem to like new people, places and things is likely to have more difficulty adjusting to changes to their sleep environment.	A baby who doesn't seem to like new people, places and things is likely to sleep better when things are predictable and may need help and gentle encouragement to get used to new things. A soothing sleep-time ritual and routine will help. The use of a transitional object (see p. 121) may help.
Adaptability	Not a baby's initial response to something new, as above, but rather how he adapts to something new *over time*.	As above, 'slow to warm up' babies may have initial difficulty with something new, but slowly adapt or adjust to it.	As above, gradual changes may help. Allowing 'slow to warm up' babies time to adjust to new things.

Table 3 continued: Temperament and its effect on your baby's sleep.

TEMPERAMENT CHARACTERISTIC	WHAT IT REFERS TO	HOW IT MIGHT AFFECT SLEEP	HOW PARENTS CAN HELP
Intensity of reaction	How intensely a baby reacts to both internal and external stimulation.	Babies with more intense reactions may be more prone to overstimulation and overtiredness.	Have a soothing bedtime ritual and routine. As above, start the wind-down time when you think your baby might be or should be getting tired; don't wait for obvious tired signs, this may mean that your baby is already overtired.
Sensory threshold	How sensitive a baby is to external stimuli such as lights, noises, etc. How easily he can shut out external stimulation.	Babies with low sensory thresholds will be more affected by loud noises, lights, uncomfortable clothing, smells, etc, and may become easily over stimulated.	Try to reduce the amount of stimulation your baby has to tolerate overall, but especially in the wind-down time and sleep time. These babies will probably do better with all-cotton clothes (labels cut out), blackout curtains and white noise machines that help minimise the external stimuli that bothers them. Realise that small upsets may really throw a more sensitive baby out of whack and they may need your help to calm down.

Table 3 continued: Temperament and its effect on your baby's sleep.

TEMPERAMENT CHARACTERISTIC	WHAT IT REFERS TO	HOW IT MIGHT AFFECT SLEEP	HOW PARENTS CAN HELP
Mood	The quality of the general mood of a baby, from positive (happy, smiling, easy to please) to negative (moody, serious, grumpy, doesn't smile easily).	The effects of mood are quite subtle and probably have more to do with how parents cope with their baby's mood and how they interact together.	Try to recognise tired signs and the effect of sleep on mood. Recognise that your baby's mood may in turn affect your mood and vice versa. If you live with someone who is a grump this will affect your mood.
Distractibility	How easily a baby is distracted from an activity or experience.	Highly distractible infants might have more difficulty feeding well and so may not take in full and satisfying feeds. They may be easily distracted from the task of falling asleep, and/or give up easily if they do not fall quickly to sleep.	If you have a distractible baby, ensure that feeding and night-time routine is free of distractions: quiet, soft lighting, no hanging mobiles, minimum movement.
Attention span and persistence	How well a baby stays with a task even if there are obstacles and/or frustrations.	Hard to say what this means for sleep. It may be that the baby persists with getting to sleep, or may be that he persists in trying to get your attention!	Be as clear as possible about expectations of the situation, if it is bedtime then sleep is what is required. Try to meet the baby's needs quickly and without fuss.

The challenges of certain temperaments

All babies need to have their needs met, but some babies need a lot more input from others to have their needs met. In fact, some babies seem to have *more needs*. These babies have come to be labeled as 'high needs' babies.[14] So-called 'high needs' babies are likely to be sensitive and intense, and may be more prone to negative moods. Such babies have also been called fussy, sensitive, spirited, demanding, inflexible, hard-to-please and plain old difficult. Various researchers say they make up four to 15 per cent of the population.[15, 16]

While no one has been able to say with confidence what makes some babies fussier, hard-to-please or difficult, it seems likely that these babies are more sensitive to sensory input than others. This means that they are more easily overwhelmed by 'normal' sights, sounds, smells around them and feelings from within their own body (such as normal bodily sensations from digestion, for example). Because these babies are so easily overwhelmed, they are also readily stressed and need more than average amounts of soothing and calming from their parents.[17] If you have a high needs baby, you are likely to need strong support as well so that you can consistently meet your baby's needs and demands.

If you think that your baby may be a high needs baby and you are wondering how on earth you will manage to get through the first year, here are some suggestions for you:

+ Spend as much time as possible with your baby, and be as patient and consistent as you possibly can.
+ Try not to take your baby's behaviour personally. Try to remember that your baby is not trying to be difficult or to annoy you, he is just having a hard time adjusting to the world.
+ Maintain a sense of humour.
+ Have a clear and consistent routine.
+ Organise a support system that gives you some breathing space (meaning time away from your baby for a break sometimes).

+ Remind yourself frequently that this phase will pass, and chances are your baby will become easier as the months go by.[15]

Other than high needs babies, the baby population is made up of 'easy' (about 40 per cent) or 'slow to warm up' (about 15 per cent) babies. The rest are a combination of all of the other categories of temperament, and don't fall neatly into any one in particular.

What else about temperaments?

The match of the infant's temperament to the parent's personality is important. This match (or *mis*-match as the case may be) may present particular rewards or challenges for you as parents. A mis-match of temperaments may happen when a baby has a very different temperament from their parent(s). For example, if you are the sort of person who loves new experiences and is bored or frustrated with routine, a baby who really needs a routine and schedule to feel safe and secure may present some challenges for you! This mis-match may result in feelings of frustration with your baby, yourself and your life as a new parent.

Case study

I used to believe that children's personalities were a direct product of the environment they grew up in, that a parent started with a completely blank canvas and developed their child over time. Now I know that that's not actually the case. What changed? I had children. Now I know that babies are born as little people with their own temperament, and some temperaments are more difficult than others! Here is how I have come to know this.

My son, Lachlan, greeted the world with a temperament somewhere between annoyed and grumpy. As a first-time mother, these traits weren't really something that I expected from any baby, let alone mine! I remember a midwife commenting on his restlessness and fiery temper a few days after his birth. This restlessness and temper still linger today, nearly three years later.

From the time we got home with Lachlan, he was difficult to comfort; he cried a lot of the time and became easily distressed when one of us didn't attend to him immediately. We had difficulty with feeding from the start and it seemed that Lachlan wasn't quite sure what he wanted most of the time. I would constantly be trying to figure out if he was hungry, tired, bored, overstimulated, needed a cuddle or even his own space for a while. He needed to be re-settled and held often, and did not like being in unfamiliar situations. It was upsetting to me that I couldn't work out what Lachlan wanted most of the time, or seem to give him whatever was needed to soothe him. I blamed my inability as a mother for his behaviour. It was a difficult time emotionally for me. Over time we found that a strict routine worked best for Lachy, and eventually we all figured it out together. These days, while Lachy is still very intense, we realise that our role as parents is to make some allowances for his temperament and help him to manage it as well.

It was a different story with our second child, Sienna, and people often comment on how very different she and Lachy are. From day one Sienna had a way of communicating that was so much easier for us to understand. Sienna cries when she needs something, whether she is hungry, needs changing or is tired. Then she stops crying when that need is met. Generally she is easy to settle and sleeps soundly once settled in her bed. She is a smiley, happy baby. She is able to adapt to different situations quite easily, and is casual and flexible. Sienna, at six months of age, is usually happy to play by herself for periods of time, and is open to interacting with a variety of people. As she grows I am noticing that her manner attracts others, and people continuously approach us to have a chat to her, which she enjoys.

Our two children are very different indeed; both are amazing kids and we love them for exactly who they are – it's going to be an exciting journey watching them develop.

Nicole, mother of Sienna and Lachlan

In a nutshell

Some temperaments present particular challenges for the development of healthy sleep habits and routines. All babies will do well with consistency and support to establish self-soothing behaviours. 'High needs' babies will take longer and need more parental input to develop their own self-soothing strategies.

Techniques to calm your baby

- holding
- gentle and rhythmic rocking your baby in your arms
- gentle and rhythmic rocking your baby in the pram or cot
- gentle and rhythmic patting of your baby's back or bottom
- gentle and rhythmic stroking (may be massage, or stroking your baby's face, arm, or head)
- wrapping (see p. 16 for diagram)
- sucking (dummy, breast, bottle)
- holding your baby in a sling or carrier
- bathing your baby in a deep warm bath may be especially calming. Make sure the water is warm not hot
- moving your baby in the pram, car or bouncer seat

- singing to your baby
- music
- white noise
- distracting your baby: change the scenery, point out something interesting such as birds outside, a mobile or toy.

The sort of settling or calming techniques that babies like may vary with their age. In the early weeks touch and physical closeness to the parent is a very useful settling technique. As your baby develops over the first year, other settling techniques become useful, such as talking or singing to your baby, or distracting them with something interesting to look at.

The crying baby

Babies cry because something does not feel right to them. Crying in the first year is instinctual behaviour that lets caregivers know that something needs attending to. Until babies can move and talk, crying is probably the most important attachment behaviour that ensures that survival needs are recognised and attended to.

Your baby may cry because of:
- a sense of being overwhelmed in the early weeks of life. This is particularly true for babies who may have had a stressful time in-utero, had a difficult birth, have a medical complication, or have the sort of temperament that means they have a low sensory threshold (see p. 25 for more on temperament)
- hunger or thirst
- tiredness or overtiredness
- the need for comfort or closeness
- discomfort, such as feeling too hot or too cold, or having uncomfortable (or dirty) nappy or clothes
- being over-stimulated
- illness or pain, from nappy rash or wind, for example.

Myths about why babies cry

There is an old wives' tale that says that a baby needs to cry to let off stress at the end of the day. In fact there is no evidence to support this idea, and researchers have actually shown that when a baby cries without comfort, and without help to cope with their distress, they can easily become overwhelmed. When this happens, their levels of the stress hormone cortisol increases.[16] Therefore, in the early months, crying babies need help to calm down and this, in turn, assists in the regulation of cortisol (the stress hormone). Parental proximity to the baby helps regulate the baby's cortisol until they are able to regulate it themselves (starting from about three to four months of age for most babies).

Another myth is that babies cry deliberately to manipulate parents into doing something they want. Research into brain development tells us that crying 'deliberately' is not possible for infants until at least eight months of age.[18] Babies cry because they need something, and crying is instinctual behaviour that babies do not have control over for most of the first year. Crying is a way of communicating, or a signal that something does not feel right.

It is true that some babies cry more than others for no obvious reason, and also that it is easier to 'read' the needs of other babies, and to comfort, soothe and calm them.

our thoughts

As a baby gets older, the different crying signals usually become easier for parents to understand. For example, parents may start to notice that the 'I'm hungry' cry sounds rhythmic and repetitive, while the 'I'm fed up' cry is louder and more prolonged. A cry that indicates that a baby is in pain usually starts quite suddenly, is persistent, high pitched, and is often punctuated by breaks of breath holding.[18] Going to a crying baby will, over time, help parents figure out what the different cries mean. This builds your confidence as a parent as well as your baby's trust.

Handling a crying baby can be very difficult, especially when it is not clear why the baby is crying. A parent's natural instinct is to protect their baby from pain, hunger and discomfort, and so the crying is *designed* to get a parent's attention, and to spur them into action. This can feel really awful if you simply do not know what is wrong or what to do.

What you can do

Try to sort out anything obvious that may be wrong and causing the crying (see list on p. 34).

Once you have addressed any or all of the above:
+ Try your baby's favourite calming technique for 10–15 minutes and listen to see if there is a change in the crying – is she starting to wind down? (See p. 33 for ideas of calming strategies.)
+ If not, you can try another calming technique for 10–15 minutes if you are still feeling calm and in control of your emotions.
+ If, after the 15 minutes or so, there is still no change in the tone of the crying, it is okay to *stop trying* for a brief time.

You may want to:
+ Sit quietly with your baby in a very quiet, darkened room (but not pitch-black). Face your baby away from you, and continue to hold her still, or gently rock her until she quiets herself. This is only recommended if you are feeling calm and have not reached a point of feeling angry or frustrated with the baby or the situation.
+ Wrap your baby and place her in a darkened (not pitch-black) room in her bed. If you're feeling calm about the crying you could sit or stand nearby occasionally saying something calming like 'You're okay, Mummy's here', sing a song, or place your hand on your baby or gently pat her in a slow and rhythmic way.

White noise (a meaningless background noise like a fan or a radio off station) or relaxing music may help calm your baby, and may make the crying seem a little less intense for you.

+ Carry your baby in a sling and get on with whatever you want to get done. Put headphones with music on if the crying is getting to you and you need time out.

Tips for staying calm

If at any point during your baby's prolonged, seemingly inconsolable crying you start to feel out of control, overwhelmed with anger, frustration or exhaustion or if you are starting to feel as though you are 'at the end of your tether' you could:

+ Put your baby in the pram and go out for a walk.
+ Get yourself and the baby in the car (if you feel able to drive), and go and visit someone supportive.
+ Put the baby safely in their bed, put on some soothing music or some white noise and leave the baby for a few minutes while you leave the room to calm down by drinking a cup of tea, exercising (e.g. skipping or yoga), or calling a family member, friend, or helpline for support.

If you are feeling very angry or frustrated, your baby is more likely to be able to calm down if she is given a chance to do this on her own away from your strong feelings (in a safe place like her bed).

It is very normal to feel overwhelmed at some point when caring for a tiny and very heavily dependent baby but if you find that you are frequently feeling stressed, upset, frustrated and out of control talk to a friend, family member or health professional (such as a GP, early childhood nurse, paediatrician or psychologist).

What to do if your baby won't stop crying

If your baby's crying persists for days or weeks and there seems to be nothing you can do to soothe her, try the following:
+ Organise for your baby to be checked (again?) by a health professional with an interest in children, such as a GP, paediatrician, early childhood nurse, or allied health professional. If you don't agree with something someone says or something does not seem right for you and your family you may want to get another opinion.
+ Speak with other parents about what might be going on.
+ Ask for some support from family, friends or professionals (or all three). Tell them, 'My baby cries a lot for no apparent reason, no matter what I do, and I could use some help at the moment.'
+ Get some help with household chores. (See Part 3, Taking care of yourself.)
+ Take a break from your baby by organising someone to look after her for a while.
+ Think ahead – this baby will not always be a crying baby. Before long she will be starting school!

It is important to note that, while all parents are likely to find a constantly crying baby difficult, those with certain temperaments will find a crying baby especially difficult to cope with. Those:
+ who are used to pleasing others and making others happy, who hate upsetting people or 'letting people down'
+ who have difficulties putting up with strong or negative feelings (in themselves or other people)
+ who like to be organised and are used to having a fair degree of control over their lives (who now find that they can't control this situation no matter how hard they try).

If any – or all – of these sorts of personalities sound like you, and you have a baby who cries a lot, it is especially important that you find supportive people to help you through this challenging time, either with practical help, or by listening to you talk about the difficulties you are facing.

Why would your baby cry a lot?

- Temperament (see more about this on p. 25).
- Persistent hunger (not getting enough milk for example). If you are worried that your baby is not getting enough milk and may be hungry please consult your doctor or early childhood nurse for advice.
- Illness, pain, or discomfort.
- Colic (see below for more information).

What is colic?

Colic sounds like a medical diagnosis that may explain what is wrong with a baby, but in fact it is a descriptive term referring to any baby who cries excessively for no apparent reason. Excessive crying is defined by the 3-rule: crying for *at least* three hours per day, three days a week for a period of longer than three weeks.

Colic usually starts around six weeks of age and stops at about three to four months (although it can continue for longer in some babies) and occurs in about one in five babies. All babies seem to grow out of colic by the six-month mark.

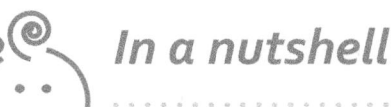 *In a nutshell*

Colic is not a diagnosis of a physical problem, although it is sometimes talked about as if it is.

There are many theories around why babies are 'colicky': gas or wind in the bowel, discomfort due to particular foods the breastfeeding mother has eaten, food allergies or intolerances, and/or pain and discomfort from other sources. There are a number of products available based on these theories, including special dummies and bottles which claim to minimise the intake of air and medicines that claim to relieve the discomfort of trapped wind. Some midwives stress the importance of getting rid of wind after a feed in 'colicky babies' and others are of the opinion that excess feeding (as in short, frequent feeds) may contribute to tummy pains and an unsettled baby. If you have been trying frequent feeds as a way to calm your baby and it doesn't seem to be working you may want to wait at least two and a half hours between feeds by using other calming techniques in between.

Talk to your GP or early childhood nurse if you would like more information.

Tips for handling colic

ANY OF THE CALMING TECHNIQUES LISTED ON P. 33 MAY HELP WITH A COLICKY BABY.

Colicky babies tend to be more unsettled and cry more in the late afternoon and early evening. You can prepare for this, and make your life a bit easier, by:

+ preparing the evening meal earlier in the day
+ enlisting help with chores at this time of day
+ planning to wear your baby in a sling at this time of the day (try putting him in the sling *before* he becomes unsettled, as part of your normal routine and see if this helps)
+ playing music to calm you and the baby (and drown out the crying a bit!).

How to tell if your baby is unwell

It is beyond the scope of this book to go into detail about the various illnesses and ailments that may affect your baby in the first year. Nonetheless we felt that it was important to include information about how to tell if your baby is unwell as this is a common cause of concern for parents in the first year.

Illness can affect your baby's sleep and, perhaps just as importantly, your concern and worry about whether or not your baby is unwell affects how you respond to them at night. Your baby cannot tell you if something aches or hurts and parents are left to wonder, guess and make the best decisions they can with the limited information they have.

Common illnesses or issues that may temporarily affect your baby's sleep are painful nappy rash, the common cold, respiratory viruses, a cough, ear infections, tummy upsets such as vomiting and diarrhoea, and teething.

Apart from the obvious signs of illness (such as a snotty nose, a cough, diarrhoea, vomiting) other signs of illness may include:

+ a higher than usual temperature (37.2°C underarm temperature; 37.5°C on her forehead). It is a wise idea to invest in a reliable thermometer (such as one that you place in the baby's ear), as this is likely to save you a lot of worry about taking temperatures
+ general grumpiness
+ crying or whinging, particularly if it is out of character or not helped by strategies that usually help
+ loss of appetite, or crying when trying to feed
+ increased night waking
+ lethargy (not as active or as interactive as usual)
+ fewer wet nappies
+ restlessness.

Consult your doctor for advice on any of these symptoms, or if you are at all unsure or worried.

Babies with the common cold who suck a dummy may wake more during the night than those who do not use dummies because a blocked nose makes it very difficult to suck and breathe at the same time, forcing your baby to spit out the dummy in order to breathe. Of course then they want the comfort of sucking and, until they can put it in themselves, this means that the parent will be up and down putting the dummy in several times a night!

Common medical issues and night waking

There are medical issues that may be related to more *ongoing* difficulties with sleeping (that is, not just a night or two here or there). These are:

Recurrent ear infections
Researchers have found a link between recurrent ear infections and sleep problems in babies.[13] This is because fluid in the ear, even if the fluid is not infected, may cause your baby to feel uncomfortable when he is lying down. If your baby has persistent difficulties with sleep and you cannot seem to figure out why, it is a good idea to ask the doctor to check his ears for excess fluid, and/or infection.

Gastro-oesophageal reflux (GOR)
Reflux occurs when the valve at the bottom of the food pipe doesn't close properly, so the milk that goes into the tummy doesn't stay in there as it should but comes back up into the food pipe (and sometimes all the way back up into the mouth and out again!). Many babies have immature gastro-oesophageal valves and 'spilling' or regurgitating is common. Thankfully the function of the valve improves over time as a baby develops

and grows and the reflux then lessens. However, researchers have found a link between reflux and sleep problems in babies.[5] It is not clear whether these sleep problems are because of the pain or discomfort caused by the reflux, or because of the small snacking feeds that babies with reflux tend to prefer.

Reflux occurs when the valve at the bottom of the food pipe (the oesophagus) is not working properly (usually due to immaturity), allowing the milk and stomach acid to come back up from the stomach into the oesophagus. This can often (but not always) lead to vomiting or spilling and painful burning in the oesophagus (caused by the stomach acids). It is not clear why some babies experience pain and discomfort with the regurgitation, and others do not, but it may be that babies with a low sensory threshold (see Temperament and sleep on p. 26) experience more discomfort than others.

our thoughts

Is it true that you should never 'let' your baby cry?

You don't always have a choice! Consider this:

+ Some crying is probably inevitable. Sometimes parents can soothe their distressed baby, sometimes they can't.
+ Crying is a necessary human attachment behaviour (see Attachment, p. 53).
+ Crying is communication and actually helps you to get to know your baby. In this sense it is not something that needs to be avoided at all costs.

Gastro-oesophageal reflux can be difficult to diagnose, as sometimes it is silent (this essentially means the valve is not working properly and discomfort or pain may be there, but there is no vomiting).

Babies with reflux usually hate lying flat on their backs or their tummies (as these positions encourage the milk and stomach acids to spill into the oesophgaus).[10] They may cry persistently and with apparent pain when they are laid down for sleep, and symptoms are often worse 30 to 60 minutes after a feed. Being upright may help as gravity helps to keep the milk and acids down. Babies with reflux may also find their 'tummy time' exercise painful and may always cry when placed on their tummy.

If you suspect that your baby has reflux consult your doctor, paediatrician and/or early childhood nurse who will help you with a diagnosis and management techniques.

In the meantime you could try:

+ keeping your baby upright for at least 30 minutes after her feed (you could put her in a sling)
+ allowing at least two hours between feeds to allow the stomach to empty
+ using bed blocks to slightly raise one end of her cot (so she is lying a little upright)
+ giving your baby a dummy, which may provide some relief as the sucking may help clear the oesophagus of acid[6]
+ consulting an allied health professional in addition to your doctor or nurse.

Gastro-oesophageal reflux occurs quite frequently in babies due to immaturity of their gastro-intestinal tract.

Part Two
The Sensible Sleep Solution

What is it?

The Sensible Sleep Solution (SSS) is a middle-of-the-road, gentle approach for helping your baby develop good sleep habits over the course of their first year. It is intended to support and give confidence to parents who do not want to leave their baby to cry in distress or to end up with the baby in the parental bed against their wishes.

The SSS has been developed by incorporating important information about brain development, attachment theory, self-soothing and sleep routines and rituals and by listening to parents as they share with us the difficulties they face when trying to make decisions about their baby's sleep. We stress the importance of your baby developing self-soothing skills throughout their first year, and show you how to help your baby learn these skills through Creating Opportunities To Self-Soothe (COTSS) at each age. See Part 4 for more information on COTSS.

Case study

My young baby hated to have her nappy changed. She would scream and flail because the nappy change seemed a new and upsetting experience for her. I needed to help her get over her discomfort. That is, I needed to teach her to 'self-soothe' during that time. I would start with active strategies, such as holding and cuddling. I would talk or sing calmly. She would get calm again when clothed and wrapped and close to me but gradually she became more used to nappy changes and less reliant on my help to calm her during the process. When I realised that she was learning a self-soothing skill it made it easier to understand why she was reacting this way – and also easier to put up with!

Jenny, mother of Mia

 **In a nutshell**

The Sensible Sleep Solution is a developmentally sensitive, supportive and gentle method of encouraging your baby to sleep and increasing your confidence as parents.

 *our thoughts*

The Sensible Sleep Solution, which uses the COTSS techniques for calming and settling, does not recommend leaving a baby to cry in distress.

Self-soothing

The ability to self-soothe is important for your baby's sleep.

You may be thinking of 'self-soothing' in terms of a baby being able to fall asleep without parental help. In fact, psychologists understand self-soothing as being more than just a baby's ability to fall sleep without help. They see self-soothing as the ability to calm and comfort oneself in the face of difficulties and emotional upsets both in the day, and at night. Babies, children and adults all need self-soothing skills. Babies and children learn the skills to self-soothe in the same ways they learn other skills – over time and with encouragement and support from others.

For children who are temperamentally calm (see Table 3, p. 26) the skill of self-soothing will be learnt earlier and with less parental input (though as toddlers and older children they will still need parental help soothing themselves in certain situations). Children who are temperamentally more highly strung will need more consistent and constant parental input and patience as they gradually learn the skills to calm themselves down after an upset. It is interesting to note that parents do not need to protect their baby from all discomfort (which is impossible anyway), they just need to help their baby learn to calm themselves down after an upset.

For self-soothing to develop over the course of the first year of life, it is important that parents don't immediately jump in to help their baby as soon as an upset occurs – this may get in the way of the development of self-soothing skills. Watch your baby for a few seconds or minutes after an upset and see if she is getting increasingly upset, or if she is finding ways to calm herself down. If she is growing increasingly distressed, go and help her calm down and look for another opportunity to watch her after an upset a few days or weeks later. Some babies place their fingers or fists in their mouth to self-soothe, older children may use a comfort toy or blanket or even twirl their hair to calm themselves down.

The Sensible Sleep Solution and controlled crying
(Sometimes called 'teaching a baby to sleep' or 'controlled comforting'.)

There are different methods that come under the banner of 'controlled crying' but they share a general principle: *leaving a baby alone to cry for various and increasing lengths of time until they fall asleep.*

The Sensible Sleep Solution acknowledges that crying cannot be avoided at certain points in a baby's development. However, our approach doesn't recommend allowing your baby to cry in distress. Instead of attending to your baby at fixed times (as in controlled crying) the SSS recommends that parents attend to their baby before they become distressed. Importantly, the Sensible Sleep Solution also focuses on Creating Opportunities To Self-Soothe, COTSS, (see Part 4) throughout the first year.

We recognise that at some point in the second half of the first year of their life some babies may cry while winding down for sleep at one point or another.

This is okay when:
- + all your baby's needs have been met, and it is reasonably clear that she is crying because she is resisting sleep
- + she is healthy and well
- + she has the ability to self-soothe in some way (such as suck her thumb, cuddle a favourite toy, suck a dummy)
- + she has not been left to cry without some assistance if she does become distressed. (For more information, see COTSS, p. 112.)

We do not believe, from the research we have done, that leaving your baby to cry himself to sleep in the early months is advisable, not only because it is distressing for the baby but also because:
- + the theory behind controlled crying (reward and learning) simply does not make sense for human babies (see p. 62 on learning)
- + babies in the first months of life are too young to genuinely learn how to get to sleep and remember how, so in all likelihood it will be necessary to teach them to sleep again at a later stage.

The theory behind controlled crying is based on two ideas. First, the more a behaviour is reinforced, or rewarded, the more it will occur. For example, the more a baby is picked up when they cry the more they will cry (because they like being picked

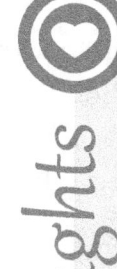

our thoughts

An important point to consider is this: while the impact of controlled crying on a baby's emotional development is not known and probably never will be, we do know that chronic lack of sleep in Mum or Dad (or both!) can contribute to family stress and parental depression or anxiety, all of which may come to negatively impact on the baby.[19]

If a parent is stressed, not coping well, or is suffering from depression or anxiety, it is possible that, for that family, in those circumstances, a version of controlled crying (i.e. letting a child cry themselves to sleep) may benefit the whole family (baby included).

If the ongoing broken sleep is really getting you down, and you are worried about how you or your family is coping, we recommend that you talk to a health-care professional about all the options available to you (and controlled crying is one of them). Remember that no family is the same and no two babies are the same – it is important that any solution you come up with fits your family's circumstances.

up). Second, if the reward (picking up) is stopped, the behaviour (the crying) will also stop. Thus if a baby is not picked up when they cry the crying will stop because the behaviour (crying) was not rewarded.

The theory behind this is based on many years of research, in humans and animals, but when it comes to use in babies, the following assumptions are *not* based on evidence:
+ Crying is a problem behaviour, and that it is essentially without cause or meaning.
+ Wanting a reward is the reason a baby cries.
+ The baby seeks reinforcement or reward just for the sake of it, not because they have a real need. In other words that babies cry on purpose to manipulate their parents.
+ The baby can learn not to cry.
+ If a baby stops crying because he was not attended to, there was either no reason for the crying in the first place, or that reason went away.

What we *do* know, based on research:
+ There is no direct evidence that controlled crying harms babies in the short or long term. It can't be researched properly because so many other things are involved in a child's upbringing that it would be very difficult to say for certain whether or not controlled crying was a cause of anything good or bad in a baby's life.
+ There is also no evidence that controlled crying does not harm a baby for the same reason as above. But leaving a child to cry unattended will result in higher cortisol levels, which indicates higher stress,[19] and falling asleep is difficult when you are stressed, even for an adult.
+ Responding promptly to babies when they cry is helpful for their developing sense of security.[16] Crying is how infants and babies communicate they need something. In the early weeks and months this may be the need to be close to caregivers, and to receive comfort from them.

+ It is simply not possible for a baby younger than eight to ten months of age to come up with a strategy (crying) in order to 'trick' his parents into coming to him. Babies cry at this stage of development simply because something does not feel right for them, not to manipulate their caregivers (see Brain development, p. 58).

In a nutshell

In the early months babies cry because something does not feel right to them, and because they need something (whether this be a nappy change, a feed, or a cuddle from Mum or Dad), not because they are purposely planning to get their parents in the room to trick them, manipulate them or to get their own way. They are not developmentally able to do this until at least eight months of age. While parents cannot always make everything feel right for their baby (and they do not need to in order to raise a healthy and happy human) it is important to realise that a baby's cry is not without cause or meaning.

Attachment

The seed of attachment theory was planted in the 1930s and 1940s when doctors and other health professionals started to notice that babies and children who were separated from their loved ones for long periods of time (such as for hospital stays) were negatively affected.[20] These children had difficulties gaining weight, rarely smiled or babbled, were generally listless and unhappy and had difficulties giving and receiving affection like hugs and kisses. Researchers finally figured out that these problems were as a result of the children being separated from their parents and the theory of attachment was born.[15] Of course this makes perfect sense to us nowadays, and we readily accept that children do not like being separated from their loved ones, and that they get distressed if they are separated for too long. We have now come to see the basic views of attachment theory as common sense and it is hard to believe that when attachment theory was first formulated its founder, John Bowlby, was treated with suspicion and scepticism by many of his peers!

Nowadays attachment theory is a widely accepted and extremely well-researched theory. The theory has not only influenced parenting and child-rearing practices, but also social policies aimed at supporting the early attachment relationships of children.

What does 'attachment' mean?

Attachment theory was developed to explain and make sense of human relationships. The attachment process is one in which a human comes to rely on another to notice, and respond to, their needs (these needs may be physical or emotional).

Attachment is often talked about in relation to babies and children but in fact the attachment process remains important throughout life. This is because relationships remain important throughout life.

In an infant, attachment behaviours serve to ensure the primary caregiver (usually the mother) stays close by. All those endearing little behaviours like smiling, goo-ing and gah-ing, and looking into your eyes (as well as the less endearing but extremely powerful crying and clinging) are *designed* to keep you close by, tuned in and paying attention. These behaviours are instinctual, pre-programmed and vital for survival because human babies need to have someone to take care of them. In fact, attachment behaviours can be seen in every species of animal whose survival depends on parental care. There is a clear *survival need* for attachment behaviours.[18]

In a nutshell

Most babies are pre-programmed to use attachment behaviours (crying, smiling, looking at mother's face) to keep their mother close, and most mothers are pre-programmed to have the urge to want to respond to these attachment behaviours. Secure attachment requires consistent loving care and an ongoing interest in the baby's world and experiences.

Why do we care about attachment?

The way attachment develops in a baby is dependent upon how the parents respond to their baby's attachment behaviours.[20] The patterns of attachment have been very widely researched and many studies have shown that sensitive loving care of a baby is most likely to result in the development of a 'secure attachment' pattern. Secure attachment is a pattern in which the child feels confident that his parent (or parent figure) will be available, interested, responsive and helpful when needed. An infant who feels confident his needs will be responded to is then eager, excited and willing to explore the world. He knows that he will have a safe base to return to when he has finished exploring or when something overwhelms or scares him.[20]

A securely attached baby is likely to develop into a securely attached child who will be:

+ confident that others will be helpful when needed
+ growing in independence
+ growing in self-reliance when exploring the world
+ cooperative with others
+ sympathetic and helpful when others are in distress.

Sixty years ago parents were not allowed to visit their babies or children at all when they were in hospital, even when the stay was for many months at a time. To make matters worse, because hospital staff were rather obsessed with keeping the hospital environment sterile (infections could readily kill people), babies and children were cared for with minimal handling so often did not get any cuddles at all. Even in the 1950s and '60s it was typical for parents to be limited to one hour of visiting a week.[15]

What about 'attachment parenting'?

In the late 1980s and early '90s the concept of attachment came to be linked to a certain style of parenting – 'attachment parenting' – by Dr William Sears.[13] Supporters of this parenting style advocate co-sleeping, baby-wearing (carrying the baby in a sling for most of the time) and extended breastfeeding, as well as 'connecting' early with the baby, and reading and responding to baby's cues. In reality the first three of these parental behaviours have little to do with the scientific theory of attachment, although great emphasis is placed on them in so-called 'attachment parenting'. It is important to note that there is no research to suggest that co-sleeping, baby-wearing or extended breastfeeding are *necessary* for the development of secure attachment and a healthy sense of self (of course they are most likely not harmful either, if parents want to do them). Babies all around the world develop secure attachments even if they do not share their parents' bed, are not 'worn' by their parents, and/or are not breastfed.

What does this mean for sleep?

You will notice in Part 2 that we talk about attachment behaviours at various ages and the impact that these may have on sleep patterns.

The main reason that we mention attachment is because it is so central for healthy child development. We are aware that other books about baby sleep either ignore attachment and the parent-child relationship totally, or promote co-sleeping as a necessary prerequisite of secure attachment and future emotional health, neither of which is supported by research evidence (or common sense for that matter).

How can secure attachment be achieved?

Promoting a secure attachment in your baby is not difficult or complicated. As babies' attachment behaviours are instinctual, so too are parents basically 'pre-programmed' to respond to their baby's attachment behaviours. This interaction is the basis of healthy attachment. For example, most parents will feel the urge to hold and cuddle their baby, to soothe her when she cries, to keep her warm and protected, to feed her when she is hungry, to smile back when she smiles, and to respond to her attempts at communication.[20] These simple and common-sense behaviours are the basis of the attachment process.

Parenting that promotes a secure attachment is warm, sensitive, responsive and dependable.[15]

 Tips for encouraging secure attachment

- Realise that you, as parent/s, are the most important people to your baby.
- Allow time to get to know your baby and wonder who he is.
- Be open to wondering what your baby is thinking, feeling and experiencing.
- Be open to the possibility that the sounds your baby makes and the things he does are a form of communication and that paying attention to them with curiosity can help you get to know him.
- Realise it takes time to understand what your baby needs, and be persistent and committed to try to gain this understanding.
- If you think or feel that your baby needs you, or if you want to attend to him in some way to reassure yourself then do so, even if others tell you that you are being silly or spoiling your baby.
- Spend time playing, reading and talking to your baby, looking at your baby's face and eyes, and cuddling and singing to your baby.
- Set aside time when you and your baby are not preoccupied or distracted and allow him the opportunity to explore your face with his eyes and, as he gets older, his hands and even his mouth if you are comfortable with this.
- If you need to leave your baby with someone else, try to ensure that that person is familiar to your baby.
- Even when your baby is very young, always say goodbye and let him know when you will be back (he may not understand the details but he will start to understand that you will always come back).
- As your baby gets older (from about 5–6 months) you can play games like 'peek-a-boo' and talk to your baby from behind a cloth or from another room. These sorts of games help babies to begin to understand that even though they can't see you, you have not disappeared.

While the urge to take care of the baby is often there for new parents, the actual details of how to take care of a baby actually need to be learnt — either by watching other parents care for their babies, from experience and spending time with babies, and/or from reading books or looking on the internet.

Brain development
Structure of the brain
Understanding how the brain develops over the first year after birth may help you understand your baby better, and make informed decisions about routine and sleep.

The brain is made up of different areas and each of these different areas has a specific function.

Brain parts
- **Brain stem** is the most developed part of the brain at birth and is responsible for basic life processes such as heart regulation, blood pressure, and breathing.
- **Cerebellum and basal ganglia** are not fully developed at birth, and are involved in the regulation and coordination of movement, posture, and balance.
- **Limbic system,** responsible for emotion and memory formation, is not fully developed at birth.
- **Cerebral cortex** is quite undeveloped at birth and is the slowest part of the brain to mature. It is also the largest part of the brain and is associated with higher brain function such as reflective thought, emotional awareness, and personality formation. The cerebral cortex has four parts, the parietal, temporal, occipital and frontal lobes. Each of these lobes is responsible for different functions (see Figure 1, p. 61) and each develops differently throughout pregnancy, the first

year, and beyond. The actual sequence of brain development seems to be more or less genetically programmed and infants all over the world progress through the same milestones at more or less the same times, despite differences in child-rearing practices.[18]

How the brain grows
A full-term healthy baby is born with all the parts of the brain that she needs to survive outside the womb. In the first few weeks your baby's spinal cord and brain stem are responsible for the instinctual reflexes (like sucking and swallowing) that are necessary for survival in the outside world. Over time, as the brain develops and matures, these instinctual actions are replaced by intentional action, organised by other parts of the brain.

Although a human infant looks like a miniature version of an adult with tiny eyes, ears, toes and nose, it is easy to see that their body does not work in the same way as those of an older child or adult. The infant's neck can't hold the head steady, the legs can't support the body to stand, and the hands can't hold onto things. In the same way, the baby's internal organs are not fully developed – the gut cannot digest solid foods, and the brain cannot think in the same way that an older child's or adult's can. One particular area of the brain,

our thoughts

Your relationship with your baby is like any other one in your life – it may have moments of perfection but it will not be perfect all the time. It will take effort, work, patience and commitment like any other relationship (with all the effort coming from the parent for the first few years!). While there will be moments of love, connection and happiness, you and your baby will also have moments of feeling bored, dissatisfied and disappointed with each other. This does not make you a 'bad' parent or your baby a 'bad' baby.

It is the overall tone or feeling between the two of you that really matters. If the general tone or feeling of the relationship with your baby is not what you would like it to be or what you think it should be, it might be an idea to talk to a trusted and understanding friend, family member or health professional about the relationship.

There is a lot that can be done to support parents in building a positive relationship with their baby.

the frontal lobe (see Figure 1), is the least developed at birth and goes on developing until we are into our twenties. The immaturity of the human brain at birth means that it is able to be influenced by life experiences and situations. This enables humans to adapt to and learn to fit into whatever environment they are born into. It is called *plasticity* of the brain.

It is important to remember that the human brain is far from fully developed at birth. In fact, it goes on developing throughout childhood, adolescence and into adulthood. In the first year of life the human brain more than doubles in weight, until it is about three-quarters of its adult weight at one year of age.

How do experiences influence the brain?
Repeated experiences actually influence the structure of the brain. At birth we have literally billions of brain cells but very few connections between these cells. Over time, with repeated experience, connections or pathways form between particular brain cells. The more a pathway is used (that is, the more an experience is repeated) the stronger the connection between those brain cells becomes. These brain connections come to influence our 'common sense' of how we see the world. For example, when a baby hears a soothing sound and at the same time feels comfortable, secure and relaxed, a connection is made in the baby's brain between the experience of the soothing sound and a feeling of relaxation. This connection gets stronger every time a soothing sound and relaxation are experienced together. Over time, the association is then established as a neural pathway on the brain and will 'kick in' every time a baby hears a soothing sound. This particular baby will come to 'just know' that sound can be soothing.

1. **Frontal lobe** – reasoning, planning, parts of speech, movement, emotions, and problem solving

2. **Temporal lobe** – perception and recognition of auditory stimuli, memory, and speech

3. **Occipital lobe** – visual processing

4. **Parietal lobe** – movement, orientation, recognition, perception of stimuli

5. **Brain stem** – responsible for basic life processes: heart rate regulation, blood pressure and breathing

Figure 1

Another example is touch. If a baby has the repeated experience of being massaged, and at the same time feeling safe and comfortable this will become a pathway in their brain and they will eventually have an understanding that being touched is a good experience. If a baby has the unfortunate experience of feeling pain or discomfort every time they are massaged then they will eventually develop the understanding that touch is not a good experience and may shy away from it, but without realising why.

How do babies learn?
Learning is a complex human task that goes on as long as we live. The definition of learning is the acquiring of information as a result of experience.[18] By this definition babies are learning all the time, and we have seen above how repeated experiences actually come to affect the way a baby's brain develops.

Conditioning is another way that babies learn in the first year, and repeated experience is involved in learning by conditioning as well (see p. 63 for explanation of conditioning). Research shows that babies are able to store simple pieces of information for short periods of time in the first six months or so, via the conditioning process.

When babies are about eight or nine months of age there is a big leap in the development of the brain and the way they learn becomes much more complex. Research shows that the first signs of 'recall memory' are seen at eight to nine months. Recall memory is the brain's ability to intentionally call up information, without any prompt being necessary. It is the ability to not only store information, but also to call on that information as needed. Recall memory is the sort of memory that allows us to think of people even when they are not physically with us.

What does this mean for sleep?
Information on brain development and how babies learn is important for parents to consider when making decisions about teaching their baby to sleep (and expectations of baby sleep) in the first year. The Sensible Sleep Solution position is that parents play a vital role in encouraging and supporting healthy sleep habits in their baby's first year and it is these (healthy sleep habits) that can be supported *over the course of the first year*.

Table 4: Learning throughout the first year (and what this means for sleep!).[17]

TYPE OF LEARNING	AGE	WHAT THIS MEANS FOR SLEEP
Neuronal connection, from repeated experiences	Begins in-utero and continues into adolescence.	Repeated experience matters. The sorts of repeated experiences that are important for the development of healthy sleep habits are: + routine/ritual around bedtime/going to sleep + having needs met + going to sleep feeling relaxed and calm + the experience of being able to calm oneself.
Classical conditioning	Begins in-utero (from about 6 months gestation)[18] and continues throughout life.	This sort of learning can be used to develop healthy, soothing sleep habits by association. For example, pair a lullaby toy with a relaxed and sleepy baby a number of times, and after a while the lullaby toy will bring the relaxed feeling to your baby.
Operant conditioning	Evident from 2–3 months of age and continues into adulthood.	Your baby's brain is starting to make some links between his spontaneous behaviours (actions without intent – like squealing) which bring results anyway (like Mum or Dad picking him up!). When your baby is very young this sort of learning only lasts a few hours. It may seem as though your baby is trying to 'trick' you to get you to pick him up but he's not – he's just experimenting with the very early stages of understanding cause and effect.
Intentional memory storage and recall of information	From about 8–10 months, continuing into adulthood.	Your baby is now really learning about cause and effect, and starting to learn that certain behaviors get results! He may now start to call out intentionally (rather than instinctually) to get you to pick him up.

The most famous example of classical conditioning is Pavlov's dogs. In this experiment, Pavlov (the researcher) rang a bell every time he gave some food to the dogs. Eventually they learned to associate the bell with food and the dogs salivated at the sound of the bell, without any food actually being around. This is a powerful method of learning and helps explain how babies begin to understand and learn about their world.

 ## In a nutshell

- **The circadian rhythm (the body's natural sleep-wake cycle) starts to develop from about two to four months of age. Before this rhythm is developed, a routine may be difficult to establish (see p. 118 for tips on how to support the development of this rhythm).**
- **Repeated experiences affect the structure of the brain, which comes to affect an individual's world view.**
- **It is not possible for a young baby to intentionally cry in order to manipulate their parents or get their attention until at least eight or nine months of age. An infant's cry is instinctual and aimed at ensuring their survival needs are met.**
- **A young baby does not have the capacity to plan a course of action and then undertake it (for example, plan to cry to get their parent's attention). A baby that cannot self-soothe will cry to get help to calm themselves down. Crying to seek comfort is instinctive.**

Learning, controlled crying and the Sensible Sleep Solution

Evidence shows that the practice of controlled crying and learning theory do not fit (at least not in the first few months of life).

The practice of controlled crying in a young baby is based on operant conditioning (see Table 4 p. 63). This theory says that crying is a random behaviour that means nothing until it is reinforced by something positive (i.e. Mum coming). The idea is that a baby has no reason for starting to cry, and she would not continue to cry unless her cry was rewarded in some way. This is the basis of the old-fashioned idea that going to a baby when she cries is spoiling her.

This theory does not make sense for young babies. Crying in the first months of life is instinctive and necessary for survival (because it ensures that the mother stays close by). We know that crying is not a random noise that a baby just happens to make for no reason.

The Sensible Sleep Solution acknowledges that by responding to a baby's cries and meeting their needs the baby will learn, over time, to calm themselves.

our thoughts

Sensitive parenting means being aware of baby's signals and responding promptly and consistently to his needs for food, sleep comfort and affection.[18]

Sensitive parents also recognise the times that their baby can tolerate waiting for a minute or so, and they aim to gently extend their baby's capacity for waiting, and for self-soothing, throughout the first year.

If the theory of operant conditioning applied to young babies we would expect that babies whose cries were responded to in the early months would cry more at 12 months of age, because their cries were 'rewarded'. In fact, research shows that babies whose cries were consistently responded to in the early months actually cried less at 12 months of age.[15]

At about eight to ten months of age, babies do start to piece together their action and a consequence (such as crying and Mum coming). As far as we can tell from research, this is the earliest that a baby can intentionally behave in a certain way in order to get something they want.

Routines and rituals

There is a lot of conflicting advice about the importance of routine in a baby's life. Like a lot of areas in parenting advice, there seems to be a lot of all-or-nothing information. In other words, the advice seems to be parents should *either* follow their baby's lead all the time (thereby ignoring the practicalities of this) *or* they follow the clock all the time (thereby ignoring their baby's cues).

The position taken in the Sensible Sleep Solution is that a routine is helpful for most babies, children and families, but that a routine does not have to be (and in fact often cannot) be forced upon a baby in the first few months of its life. In this book we offer recommendations on how to develop a routine in the first year.

It is important to get to know your baby, her temperament, what she likes (and what she dislikes), what is likely to make her feel happy, grumpy and overtired. It is also important to be able to have some predictability in *your* day, and to gradually support your baby to fit into the world that they have been born into (your family).

The Sensible Sleep Solution recommends a combination of both following your baby's lead, and developing a routine. For example, a baby is not born with a set circadian rhythm (see p. 7), and so cannot know night from day. Given this, it would be unrealistic and unnecessarily stressful to try to force your baby into a day/night cycle of feeding and sleeping in the early weeks. However, it is important to note that you can take the lead in helping your baby adapt to a more socially acceptable day and night cycle. You can follow your baby's lead (a real need to feed in the middle of the night) in the early weeks, while gently encouraging him to adapt to a more convenient eating, waking, and sleeping pattern. See Part 4 for some examples of routines that might suit you.

Demand feeding

When we talk about routine we also have to consider the current debate on 'demand feeding'. The concept of demand feeding (also called cue feeding) became popular as a reaction to the so-called 'scientific method' of parenting in the 1950s when feeding babies four-hourly, and making them wait for their milk (even if they were crying) was the standard advice. Demand feeding involves noticing when a baby is hungry and feeding them, even if the four hours is not up.

Over time the concept of demand feeding has become a little confused and sometimes seems to

our thoughts

Of course it makes sense to feed your baby when you think she is hungry (i.e. showing signs of hunger) as opposed to when the clock says she should be hungry. This is the essence of what is meant by demand feeding. But deciding to use the demand feeding approach does not have to mean that feeding (or offering the breast) becomes the one and only way of settling or calming your baby.

The Sensible Sleep Solution promotes responsive and sensitive parenting which aims to understand what a baby's needs are at any given time. Of course her need is not always for a feed, and it is possible to ignore or mistake her actual need by assuming that she is hungry and offering the breast or bottle whenever she is crying or unsettled.

A degree of routine or regulation during the days usually makes for more relaxed babies and parents because predictability is important for us all.

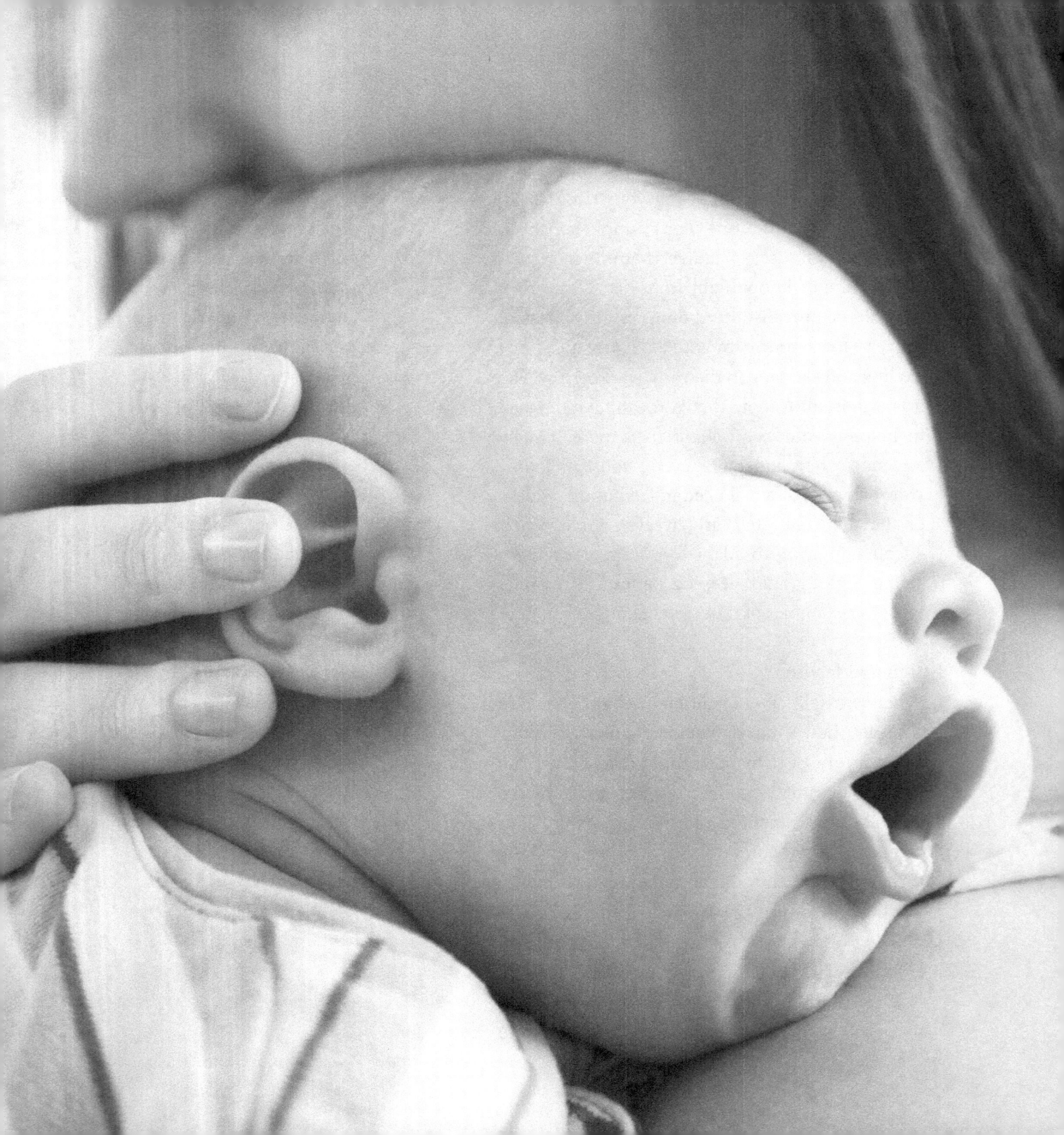

now be (mis)understood as meaning that a baby is fed, or offered the breast, *whenever she cries or shows signs of discomfort, regardless of whether or not that discomfort is caused by hunger.* This is not what was initially meant by demand feeding, and it is very important to remember how very different the parenting culture of today is from the 1950s.

Infant development and routine
A routine with a newborn may be difficult to establish because they:
+ have difficulty waiting for what they need
+ have not developed a circadian rhythm.

With most babies, following a routine is not possible for the first couple of months.
As time goes by two things start to happen that make a routine easier to establish.
+ The baby's needs become more predictable and apparent to the parent.
+ A pattern to the day starts to naturally emerge with the development of the circadian rhythm.

Case study

> *I had a very structured routine from day one. I allowed the routine to evolve as the babies have grown. They know when its bath time, dinner time, time to get dressed. They have a sense of predictability which I believe brings security and it has helped my husband and I to manage our working lives and our family lives successfully. We too like to know what's going to happen next!*
>
> *Marni, mother of twins*

Part Three
Taking care of yourself

Coping with less sleep

While we acknowledge that there are some stay-at-home or single dads out there, the reality is that women are still more likely to be doing the lion's share of caring for an infant in the first few weeks, and so this section is aimed at mums mostly. However, the information below can still be helpful for dads!

Many women are already tired when they start their life as a mother. Pregnancy, poor sleep late in pregnancy, and then the (often difficult and maybe during the night) task of labour, and a hospital stay, all contribute to tiredness before the baby even arrives home. While many women expect to feel tired for the first few weeks after the birth, most do not realise that tiredness may go on and on for weeks to months. Few new mums have the opportunity to catch up on lost sleep anytime in the first year.

Sleep for new parents is a serious issue. Sleep deprivation can contribute to irritability, anxiety, poor concentration and low mood in mothers *and* fathers. Perhaps not surprisingly, some researchers have found that ongoing sleep deprivation can contribute to the onset of post-natal depression.[20] Given this, it is important that all parents plan in advance, as best they can, how they are going to manage the interrupted sleep that comes hand in hand with parenthood.

Taking good care of yourself can help you cope with less, or poorer quality sleep than usual.

Diet

Some women feel pressure to lose their 'baby weight' very quickly. Losing weight quickly is not easy for most women, especially after a pregnancy and with the demands of a new baby, yet the pressure from society is very real.

Many women are tempted to eat less or even follow a fad diet (such as 'low carbs') to lose weight quickly. It is important to bear in mind that low carbohydrate diets were not designed for the woman getting up to feed a baby in the night, a task which takes an enormous amount of energy. Poor eating is likely to contribute to low energy levels which make it difficult to cope with the demands of a new baby.

Here are some ideas to consider:
+ Eat a balanced diet, including protein and carbohydrates at all meals.
+ Eat healthy snacks when you feel hungry. Have them ready to go in the fridge or cupboard.
+ Drink at least a litre of water a day, more if you are breastfeeding.

Exercise

Exercise has been shown to enhance well-being and reduce depression by releasing feel-good hormones called endorphins. 'Exercise' does not have to mean going to the gym, or anything that takes that much organisation. Consider the following exercises:
+ going for a walk with your baby in the pram or a sling
+ increasing 'incidental activity' (e.g. choosing stairs instead of elevators, walking instead of driving for short trips, parking away from the shops etc).

Rest and relaxation

Organise time for rest and relaxation at least once or twice a week. Allowing time for sitting watching some television, reading a book, or listening to a relaxation or meditation tape will help you cope with less sleep in the long term.

The standard advice when one has a new baby is to sleep or rest when the baby does and to go to bed when the baby does at night. Some women find this works for them. If so, great! Other mums find that this advice does not suit them for a number of reasons, such as:
+ they can't get to sleep on cue (even when they are really tired)
+ they want or need to spend this time differently, such as working, studying, caring for other children, washing, ironing, gardening, being with their partner, or relaxing in some other way

- they may find being woken (yet again) by their baby simply too frustrating to bear, and this can contribute to feelings of anxiety or depression.

Here are some other tips if the 'standard advice' does not work for you.
- Plan to rest or sleep once or twice a week – perhaps on a day that someone else can go to your baby when she wakes.
- If you can, go for a sleep when the baby does during the day, but set an alarm so that it is this, not the baby, that wakes you. If there is time after your nap you can get on with some other things that need doing or sit and relax while you wait for your baby to wake.
- Go to bed when your baby does every second night or at least a couple of times a week.
- Plan to sleep-in on a weekend or day that someone else can go to your baby in the morning. Perhaps on that day your partner or other support person can bring the baby to you for a feed and then you can get some more rest.
- A 20-minute nap has been shown to be very beneficial and can help you get through the more demanding parts of the day.[21]
- Allow others to help out practically. Many women find asking for or accepting help difficult, probably because they are used to not needing help or maybe because they think they shouldn't need it. It is interesting how we tend to romanticise some aspects of non-Western culture's baby-rearing practices (such as co-sleeping and carrying a baby in a sling) but fail to recognise that women in these cultures are able to undertake such practices because of extensive support from other women and an entirely different set of expectations of women and families. Think of the saying 'it takes a village to raise a child'. Accept help. Ask for help.

Housework

The standard advice is to let the housework go a little. Some parents find this works for them. Other parents do not appreciate this advice, for a number of reasons, such as:
+ they are used to having their house look a certain way and this is important to them
+ not having a tidy house contributes to feelings of being out of control for them
+ others people's opinions of how their house looks matters to them.

Here are some tips.
+ Try to accept that the house may not always look as good as it once did, and this is because your circumstances have changed.
+ Remember that how your house looks is not a reflection of how good you are as a mother or as a woman.
+ There is a middle ground between constantly spotless and totally feral. Think about this: someone will always have a messier house than you, and someone will always have a cleaner house than you. Be realistic.
+ Do jobs when you can see they need doing, not just because you would normally do them on a given day.
+ Keep one room or area tidy, so that you feel comfortable about inviting people around at short notice (anxiety about how the house looks, and what other people may think about it can contribute to social isolation for some mums).
+ For jobs that are getting on top of you, get some help. For example, ask your partner, mother or someone else to do one or two of the jobs that you can't seem to get to or you really hate.

Partnership/Relationship

If you don't have a partner living with you, do all you can to ensure that you build up a support network that provides you with practical help as well as emotional support for the parenting journey ahead.

If you do have a partner, talk, talk, talk all along the way about how you are both going and how you can support *each other*. It is very easy to get into competition with each other in the first year, about who is more tired, who does more, who works harder, who is busier. Being in competition doesn't allow much room for supporting each other, or for recognising what each of you is doing well and what each of you is struggling with. Try acknowledging that you are *both* tired, busy, stressed and working hard to meet your *common goals* and ask each other, 'What would make our lives a bit easier/less stressful at the moment?'

Balancing your baby's needs with your own

Babies are very demanding of their parents' physical and emotional energy. Sometimes things such as relationship problems, mental health issues (like depression or anxiety), grief, or physical illness make the tasks of parenting even more difficult. Babies simply cannot take anyone else's needs into consideration, think about how another person may be feeling, or control their behaviour to suit another person.

It is important to remember that:
+ the parents' emotional needs must be met as much as possible so that they can focus on taking care of their baby, and
+ it is all right for parents to accept help and support from friends, family or professional services.

How are you going?

It can be very difficult to know if what you are feeling and experiencing is 'normal', especially with a first baby. It can also be very difficult to know if you are doing an okay job or not, especially if there is no one around to tell you.

A good tip is to think back over the past month and ask yourself if, in your new role in life, you have:

+ enjoyed the past month for most of the time?
+ felt as though you were in control and coping for most of the time?
+ felt as though you did a good job looking after your baby for most of the time?
+ still managed to see the funny side of things and enjoy things you usually would most of the time?

If you haven't *mostly* enjoyed your life, and felt as though you were coping for *most* of the time, then extra support may be required to get you on track to being the parent you want to be. See the back of the book for information on where to get some support.

our thoughts

Your memories and experiences of childhood, and your current relationship with your parent/s are likely to influence the decisions you make about all aspects of parenting, including sleep.

One parent and child researcher[31] says that many mothers who report toddler sleeping difficulties also report that they were not well cared for as children. Why should this be so? Maybe, in their effort to be a better parent than they themselves had, some parents try to protect their own child from any sort of anxiety, distress or discomfort. In doing so, parents may end up 'over-responding' to every whimper or cry, so their baby is actually prevented from developing any tolerance to negative feelings and from learning the skills of self-soothing necessary for healthy sleep habits.

Talking through any unresolved feelings about your own childhood, and your current relationship with your parent/s, can be helpful when making decisions about how to become the parent you want to be for your own child.

In a nutshell

Ideally your own needs and your baby's needs can be met. If you feel that you can't balance this, seek help. (See Resources section in the back of book for where to get help.)

Feeling low?

Having a new baby is a time of adjustment. With so many big changes it can be hard to know what is 'normal' and what is not – with your baby, your relationship and even yourself. Below is some information on the baby blues, postnatal depression and postnatal psychosis.

The baby blues

The baby blues lasts for a few hours to a couple of days (typically occurring between days 3 and 10 after the birth) and involves feeling emotional, teary, and generally overwhelmed. Most researchers agree that the baby blues is caused by hormone changes after the birth.[22] For most new mothers, all that is needed is a bit of extra support, reassurance and understanding.

Postnatal depression

Postnatal depression affects almost 16 per cent of women in Australia.[22]

Postnatal depression is a depression that develops between one month and one year after the birth of baby. Symptoms may develop quite suddenly, or gradually over a few months. Postnatal depression can occur in any mother of any age, may occur after the first or subsequent births, and may occur after a vaginal or caesarean birth.

Symptoms of postnatal depression include:

+ low mood (feeling sad or flat) for most of the time
+ frequent crying
+ loss of interest in things that were previously enjoyed

- sleep disturbance (i.e. being unable to sleep when your baby is asleep or wanting to sleep all the time)
- feeling anxious (feeling uneasy, or a sense of apprehension or dread)
- fear of being alone (or alone with the baby)
- change in appetite
- irritability
- difficulties remembering and/or concentrating
- difficulties with decision-making
- excessive worry. For some women this worry is particularly about their own, their baby's or their partner's health
- feelings of guilt, inadequacy or inability to cope with the demands at hand
- increased physical problems, including headaches, lethargy and general aches and pains
- thoughts of suicide or death.

Of course, not all women with postnatal depression will have all of these symptoms, some will only have one or two, some will have almost all of them. Think back over the last week and ask yourself how often you have experienced any of the symptoms listed, and seek help if you are not doing as well as you would like to be. You could start by talking to your GP, paediatrician or your early childhood nurse. GPs and medical specialists can organise a referral to a psychologist or a psychiatrist as needed.

Treatment may involve counselling, practical support, and/or medication.

Postnatal psychosis
Postnatal psychosis is much rarer than either of the above two conditions, affecting 1 in 500 women in the first four weeks or so after childbirth.[22] Symptoms of postnatal psychosis include severe mood disturbance, confused and bizarre thinking (thought disturbance), seeing or hearing things that are not there (hallucinations), and believing things that are not true (delusions). Women with a personal or family history of bi-polar disorder or schizophrenia are more at risk of developing postnatal psychosis.[22] Urgent medical treatment is necessary.

Part Four
Age groups and routines

In this section, we give you month-by-month information about your baby from birth to 12 months of age: how they are developing, how that affects their sleep, and what you can do to develop healthy sleep habits in your baby.

Birth to Four Weeks

Development

Within hours of birth a baby can recognise her mother by sight, sound and smell.[12]

Vision

Although newborns can see reasonably well (particularly at close range) their vision is not fully developed at birth.

Here are some things you may notice:
+ Newborns are very strongly attracted to the sight of faces; they seem to be almost compelled to look at faces.
+ Newborns have difficulty controlling their eyes to follow a moving object.
+ Newborns can most easily see very high contrast (such as black and white), and their eyes are automatically drawn to contrast. Show your baby a bold black and white picture and watch how she is compelled to stare at it.

Hearing

Although newborns hear quite well at birth (much better than most other mammals at birth) their hearing is not fully developed. Quiet and high-pitched sounds are more difficult to hear.

Birth to Four Weeks

Touch and bodily sensations

The sense of touch is the most advanced of the senses at birth.

It is a big shock for your baby to be in the outside world for the following reasons:

+ She has moved from the warm, cosy, secure and liquid surrounding of the womb to the cool air of the outside world.
+ In the outside world her arms and legs can flail about without containment.
+ She has moved from a state of permanent satisfaction with no hunger pangs (all nutrients are provided through the umbilical cord) to the sensation of an empty tummy and needing to cry for food; and from never feeling the sensation of milk in her tummy to a tummy full of milk (maybe with air bubbles!).
+ She experiences strange and new sensations of bodily functions, such as digestion.

Because of all this newborns are easily overwhelmed. Babies can feel genuinely distressed about what seem like minor events to their parents (such as bathing or dressing), and the normal sensations that go on in their body.

Behaviour and motor skills

Babies are born with a number of reflexes. A reflex is an automatic response to nerve stimulation that is not within conscious control. Some reflexes persist throughout life (such as blinking, gag and knee-jerk reflexes). Other reflexes, like the sucking reflex and Moro reflex (which has baby throwing out her arms and legs when she experiences a sudden change to her position or if startled by a loud noise) do not persist beyond the first few months. These reflexes can affect settling to sleep and staying asleep.

Sleep

+ Newborns' brains are not mature enough to have determined sleep stages as older children and adults have. The circadian rhythm has not developed, so a newborn baby is unable to distinguish the difference between night and day.[23]
+ Newborns do not show the same patterns of REM and non-REM seen in adults. Instead they have active and quiet sleep (see p. 6 for more on this).[23]
+ About 80 per cent of an infants' sleep is 'active' sleep.[23]
+ Because active sleep is light sleep babies are woken easily from it, for example following a reflexive movement (startle) or when their tummy feels a bit uncomfortable.
+ Newborn babies are more likely to be woken by something going on within them (hunger, wind, a startle reflex) than something outside of them. This is because of a protective mechanism called habituation that newborns use to 'shut out' too much stimulation, and why many newborns seem to sleep through anything and everything going on around them. Babies differ in their ability to shut out external stimulation (see Temperament and sleep, p. 26).
+ Babies jerk, grunt, grimace and generally move a lot during their sleep. You may also notice that they have an irregular breathing pattern, which is a feature of active sleep.

Researchers who describe babies who 'sleep through the night' actually consider a five hour stretch between the hours of 11 pm and 5 or 6 am as 'sleeping through'.[24] Many babies will continue to wake at least once a night throughout the first year. This is considered normal.

Birth to Four Weeks

What to expect

+ The recommended total sleep time (in a 24-hour period) for newborns, is between 14 and 20 hours.[3, 23]
+ Your baby will only have short periods of being awake.
+ Feeding takes up a lot of time. In the early weeks each feed will take anywhere from 20 to 60 minutes.
+ Feeding and sleeping are closely related in the newborn stage. Babies need to feed little and often and so will be unable to sleep for long periods of time without needing to wake for a feed. This is because their tummies are very tiny.
+ Newborns often fall asleep at the end of a feed. Feeding can be a very tiring process for a baby (but talk to a GP or early childhood nurse if your baby is unable to stay awake long enough to take in a full feed).
+ Self-soothing behaviours (see p. 49 for more information on self-soothing) are rarely seen in newborns. Temperament (see p. 25) may help explain the existence of self-soothing skills in some infants at birth.
+ Signs of tiredness are not always obvious or easy to recognise in newborns. They include jerky movements of the arms and legs, clenched fists, frowning, yawning and crying. Infants differ in how clearly they show tired signs. Babies are temperamentally different in how easy (or difficult!) they are to 'read'.
+ Many newborns will be awake for an hour or so before showing some tired signs, others may become tired sooner, and a few will continue to stay awake without showing signs of being tired. Be on the lookout for signs of tiredness which may come as soon as 10 minutes after feeding, particularly if your baby takes a long time to feed.
+ Newborns are noisy sleepers – they grunt, groan, snuffle and whimper in their sleep. This does not necessarily mean they need your attention.
+ A baby's eyes will be drawn to lights and contrasts. It is best to have dimmed lights and/or lamps so your baby is not distracted by bright overhead lights.
+ Babies may be startled by loud noises in the first few weeks.

Parental challenges

From month to month throughout the first year, there will be situations that will challenge you as parents. These challenges are many and varied. We have included a list of some common challenges at each age in the sections below.

+ Recovering from labour and birth.
+ Learning about your baby. Finding out about him and his needs, and figuring out how he lets you know about these needs.
+ Interrupted sleep and lack of sleep. Dealing with the 24/7 demands of a new baby mean that many parents feel tired and overwhelmed a lot of the time.
+ Lack of certainty about what to do, or the 'right' way to do things can feel overwhelming and scary.

Practical tips

Don't stress and obsess about teaching your baby to sleep or establishing a routine at this early stage. Spend this time getting to know your baby.

+ Respond as quickly as possible to your baby's cries.
+ Set up a night-time sleep and change station, with a dim nightlight and everything you need for night feeds.
+ Some parents may want to occasionally give their baby opportunities to fall asleep on their own, without rocking, walking, feeding or any other active comforting. A few babies, from birth, are quite good at getting off to sleep without any parental help. To find out if you have one of these rare creatures you could try putting him into his bed when he is fed, content and sleepy, and see if he falls sleep. (See p. 90 on COTSS for tips to encourage this process.)
+ Wrapping may help calm your baby at this age, helping him fall sleep (see p. 13 for this).
+ Spend some time watching, and listening to your baby as she sleeps. This will help you become comfortable with all the noises your baby makes while asleep

and will hopefully reassure you they are normal, and that she does not necessarily need your attention for every snuffle or grunt.
+ It's okay to wake your baby if you think he is due for a feed.
+ Some parents choose to give their baby a dummy to help them settle. It is worth noting, if you are breastfeeding, that some midwives recommend not using a dummy while breastfeeding is being established (for the first 4 weeks or so).
+ A baby sling or carrier may be helpful for those times your baby is unsettled. Having your baby in a sling or carrier, even if for a few hours a day at this age, will not cause sleep problems now or later.
+ Painkillers such as paracetamol and ibuprofen are not recommended for infants under one month. If you suspect your baby is in pain or has a fever see your doctor as soon as possible.

Routine

For all the reasons listed above, a routine that is determined by the time of day is rarely possible for your newborn.

Here are some points on heading towards a routine.

our thoughts

When you have young babies, lots of people like to give you advice to:
+ demand feed/not demand feed
+ control cry/never control cry
+ sleep when your baby sleeps/clean the house when they sleep
+ breastfeed or the world will end and – my absolute favourite –
+ do what works for you!

How can you 'do what works for you', when you've never been in the situation before and so have no idea what works for you!

Marni, mother of twins

Birth to Four Weeks

+ Most newborns will struggle to stay awake for more than two hours. If your baby is still not showing tired signs after about 90 minutes awake (including the time taken to feed) start to wind her down to prepare for sleep before the two-hour mark. (See COTSS p. 90 for these techniques.)
+ Now is the time to start helping your baby 'learn' the difference between night and day, if you wish. Exposing your baby to filtered sunlight (while protecting his skin) in the morning and again between midday and 4 pm can help his body learn the difference between night and day. And remember to make sure night feeds are quiet and calm, without talking or games or any other stimulation.
+ Instead of a routine based on times, it is more realistic to start to develop predictable patterns of caring for your baby that will eventually help you both establish a routine, such as:
  - feeding your baby on waking, burp her (if she needs it), let her have some awake time and let her sleep when she is ready (this can be in her bed or in your arms – enjoy this stage while you can!)
  - spending some time in the sunlight in the morning, for example by going for a walk
  - giving her a bath followed by massage and then a sleep (at any point during the day – this does not have to be linked to the night-time bedtime routine yet)
  - following the COTSS routine (see p. 90) when you think it is sleep time.

The COTSS Method (Creating Opportunities To Self-Soothe) for the first three months

The following steps show you how to give your baby the opportunity to learn self-soothing skills around sleep time.

1. Start slowing and calming your activity around your baby as sleep time approaches.
2. Check that your baby's needs have been take care of (clean nappy, fed, burped etc.).
3. Take your baby to her sleep room.
4. Wrap her.
5. Give your baby her sleep aid if she has one (e.g. dummy).
6. Cuddle your baby in your arms, rock/sway/pat gently until she is very calm and or drowsy.
7. Say, 'Ssh – it's sleep time,' or whatever else you like (a short lullaby for example).
8. Put her down in the cot awake but almost asleep.
9. You can pat or rub your baby on the back for a little while if you want, and repeat your sleep words or song.
10. Leave your baby to see if she can settle to sleep on her own. Notice what she does as she gets ready for sleep. Is she showing signs of self-soothing?
11. If your baby cries, you can try to settle her with some more patting, rocking and calming words while she is in her bed.

If the crying escalates and she sounds as though she is getting distressed, repeat steps 6 to 9. You can repeat these as many times as you like until your baby is calm enough to fall asleep, but if it does not seem to be working let her fall asleep however she can and try again in a couple of days, weeks or months.

If you want your baby to fall asleep in your arms, or the pram, a sling or car seat it's fine to allow this occasionally at this stage. It's not likely to become a sleep problem just yet, so enjoy!

Birth to Four Weeks

The COTSS method suggests your baby is awake when you put them down in their bed. This may take time to achieve, and will also change between 'easy to put down awake' and 'harder to put down awake' at different points during the first 12 months.

Note that the Sensible Sleep Solution, which uses the COTSS techniques for calming and settling, does not recommend leaving a baby to cry in distress.

Table 5: Baby sleep at a glance: birth to four weeks.

WHAT TO EXPECT	TIPS
Newborns sleep a lot and most will not be happily awake for more than about 2 hours at a time.	Wrapping may help your baby settle as it prevents him from startling himself with arm movements.
Newborns tend to jerk, grunt and snuffle when they are asleep. Internal processes (like wind or hunger) are more likely to wake them than external noise or stimulation.	Don't stress or obsess about getting baby into a routine based on times of the day yet, instead start developing predictable patterns of behaviour, like bath, massage and sleep.
Feeding takes up a lot of time; feeds are frequent.	Allowing your baby some exposure to filtered sunlight during the day will help the development of their circadian rhythm.
Newborns are easily overwhelmed and may be distressed by simple things like bathing, dressing or needing a poo, all new experiences for your baby.	Use a baby sling for times that your baby is unsettled and just wants to be held.

Tips for stopping your baby falling asleep while feeding

If your baby is falling asleep while sucking at the breast/bottle or dummy, you can try removing the nipple/teat gently by breaking the suction with your little finger and seeing if she can continue to fall asleep on her own without the sucking.

Four to Eight Weeks

Development

Vision
Babies seem increasingly interested in looking at faces and their ability to focus is improving.

Thinking /feeling
Many babies start social smiling at this age. Smiling is a very important attachment behaviour[16] (see Attachment, p. 53) which serves to keep those most important to the baby close by, interested and wanting to interact.

Behaviour and motor skills
- Many babies become more wakeful, may cry more and want more frequent feeds.
- Your baby may not be ready for sleep straight after her feed.
- The sucking reflex begins to be replaced by 'intentional sucking'.

Sleep
- About 80 per cent of a baby's sleep is 'active' sleep, from which babies easily awaken.[23]
- Babies move and make a lot of noises during their sleep. You may also notice that they have an irregular breathing pattern – a feature of active sleep.
- Babies, on average, need to sleep 15–18 hours per 24-hour period.[23]
- Your baby does not yet know night from day, but with a little luck you may be starting to notice the longest period of sleep is at night.
- You may be gaining more idea of your baby's temperament by noting his sleeping behaviours – some babies will still fall asleep wherever they are if they are tired,

while others will be starting to show preferences about where and how they want to sleep.

What to expect

- Many babies can now stay awake for about two hours at a time. Your baby may spend two hours awake, followed by two to three hours asleep before being awake again for another couple of hours.
- In a 24-hour period your baby will probably be having four to six sleeps of between two and five hours in length.
- Feeding and sleeping are still closely related. Babies need to feed little and often and so will be unable to sleep for long periods of time without needing to wake for a feed. If feeding is not going well, it is very likely that this will be affecting sleep.
- Baby may still be falling asleep while feeding. This is normal.
- Tired signs at this age include jerky movements of the arms and legs, clenched fists, frowning, yawning and crying.

Practical tips

- It's still not time to start stressing about teaching your baby to sleep or getting into a routine. Continue to respond promptly to your baby's cries.
- You can expose your baby to filtered sunlight light in the waking periods (in the morning and then again between midday and 4 pm). This can help their bodies adjust to the night and day circadian system.
- Ensure that night feeds are quiet, without talking or games, with the minimum attention given.
- Some parents may want to give their baby opportunities to occasionally fall asleep on their own. (See COTSS p. 90 for how to do this if you want to try it.)
- If you are using a good quality nappy, if it is wet only you may not choose to change it at every night feed.

- Wrapping may help calm your baby, helping him fall asleep at this stage (see p. 13 on wrapping).
- It's okay to wake your baby if you think he is due for a feed.
- A baby sling or carrier may be helpful for times your baby is unsettled and does not want to be put down.

Routine

Here are some tips to start getting your baby ready for a routine.

- Some parents find that getting themselves and their baby up at the same time each day is helpful in establishing a sense of order in their day.
- Aim for 2½–3½ hours between feeds during the day. This amount of time encourages your baby to feed well, and also means that she can get about five feeds in between the hours of 7 am and 10 pm. This is nudging the baby towards a pattern of getting most of their calories during the daytime.
- Feed your baby on waking, burp her, let her have some awake time and tummy time and then help her get ready for sleep.
- Give her a bath followed by massage and then a sleep (at any point during the day – this still does not have to be linked to the night-time routine).
- Allow baby some filtered sunlight in the morning to support the development of the circadian rhythm.
- Introduce a sleep-time routine. It is not necessary to do this for every sleep at this stage, but at least once or twice a day will help establish it. (See COTSS p. 90 for how to establish a sleep routine.) It is still okay if your baby falls asleep in your arms sometimes at this point.

our thoughts

You're learning more about your baby as each day goes by. Maybe you now know what makes him laugh and what is likely to make him grumpy.

Are you finding it easy or difficult to settle him?

Some babies are becoming easier to read by now, others are still a puzzle to their parents.

Four to Eight Weeks

Table 6: Baby sleep at a glance: four to eight weeks.

WHAT TO EXPECT	TIPS
Your baby will be spending more time awake now, may cry more and will probably want more frequent feeds. Feeding may have become more efficient, with your baby taking less time to have a full feed. If feeding is not going well sleep will be affected too. Most babies can now stay awake for about 2 hours at a time. Your baby will probably be having 4 to 6 sleeps of between 2 and 5 hours length in a 24-hour period.	Wrapping may help your baby settle as it prevents him from startling himself with arm movements. At this age it may seem as though your baby doesn't like being wrapped or it may be becoming a problem if your baby is wriggling out of his wrap. This is the time to invest in a bigger wrap, or a specialised wrap that he can't get his arms out of so easily. It's still not time to be concerned about getting your baby into a routine based on times of the day yet, just continue with developing predictable patterns of behaviour (e.g. change nappy on waking, feed, play time and then settle to sleep time). Get your baby up and give him his first feed of the day at the same time each morning, this will help him move towards a more predictable routine. Allowing your baby some exposure to filtered sunlight during the day will help the development of his circadian rhythm. Use a baby sling when your baby is unsettled and just wants to be held.

See p. 90 for COTSS for this age.

Flat head
(ALSO KNOWN AS 'POSITIONAL PLAGIOCEPHALY')

Flat head, as the name implies, refers to the appearance of a flat area on the baby's head, typically at the back but it may be seen on either side of the head.

Babies skulls are soft and malleable (they need to be so that the baby's big head can squeeze out of the birth canal) and this means that they are prone to becoming misshapen. Flat head happens when there is repeated pressure on one side or part of the head, for example when a baby sleeps in the same position with his head to one side all the time.

Flat head has been seen more often over the last decade as babies have been placed on their backs to sleep in response to safety recommendations aimed at reducing the incidence of SIDS.

The standard advice offered to parents about flat head seems to be don't worry, your baby will grow out of it. Nonetheless, despite being told not to worry many parents do worry about whether something is seriously wrong with their baby's skull or brain and/or how their baby looks. When the flat head is severe, it may even affect a parent's feelings towards their baby and their willingness to socialise with other parents and babies.

So what can be done? The main consideration is to make sure that your baby is not lying with her head in the same position all the time. You can do this by:

+ alternating the head position each time you put your baby down in her bed (while ensuring she is always on her back)
+ encouraging your baby to turn her head when lying down by placing interesting things for her to look at on both sides
+ minimising the time she is lying flat on her back when she is awake. You can do this by giving her supervised tummy time, carrying her in a sling, and/or sitting her in a bouncer chair in a slightly upright position
+ alternating sides that you hold your baby when feeding. When bottle-feeding it is easy to get into the habit of feeding your baby with your dominant hand.

Of course, it is important to talk to your doctor or paediatrician if you have any concerns about your baby's health.

Eight to Twelve Weeks

Development

Vision

Your baby is starting to see more subtle contrasts than the black and white of the early weeks of life, and her eyes may not be so drawn (and fixed) to sharp contrasts.

Many babies are now able to track (follow with their eyes) a moving object. You may notice, for example, that your baby watches you moving around the room.

Thinking/feeling

- You may be starting to read your baby's temperament more clearly.
- Your baby is not capable of voluntary behaviour yet (they cannot decide to do something and then do it).
- Babies are getting used to being in the world and their stress response (the surges of the stress hormone cortisol) declines steadily from this age on. Because of this, many babies no longer get as distressed about 'minor' disruptions to their comfort, like bathing or being dressed and undressed as they did in the earliest weeks.[18]
- Many babies will now smile responsively when someone smiles at him, and may spontaneously 'mimic' exaggerated facial expressions.
- Many babies are still very interested in looking at faces.

Behaviour and motor skills

- 'Pre-speech' is becoming more frequent at this stage. This is a technical term for your baby's vocalising, a skill he needs to practise before being able to form words.
- Your baby may be able to briefly hold something in his hand (if it is placed there for him).

Eight to Twelve Weeks

Sleep

+ Active sleep has reduced from about 80 per cent to 65 per cent of an infant's sleep and there is an increasing proportion of 'quiet' sleep. You may have noticed your baby's breathing is quieter and slower now and she is starting to seem calmer while asleep.[23]
+ Development of circadian rhythm begins, and your baby's body begins to respond physiologically to night and day.[23]
+ Recommended sleep is between 14 and 18 hours per 24-hour day.[23]

What to expect

+ Your baby may spend two to three hours awake then the same amount of time asleep before being awake again for another couple of hours.
+ In a 24-hour period your baby will probably be having four to six sleeps of between two to five hours in length.
+ The longest stretch of sleep is likely to be at night. (But remember, five hours is still considered a good stretch for a baby this age.)
+ Feeding and sleeping are still closely related. Babies will be unable to sleep for long periods of time without needing to wake for a feed.
+ Breastfeeding babies are likely to wake more often at night than bottle-fed babies, because breast milk is more easily digested than formula.
+ Tired signs at this age include jerky movements of the arms and legs, clenched fists, frowning, yawning and crying.
+ Although your baby's sleep is getting calmer you may still hear grunts, groans, shuffles and whimpers. These noises do not necessarily mean that your baby needs your attention.

Eight to Twelve Weeks

Practical tips

+ You may notice a routine starting to develop in your days and nights but don't stress if it is not there yet.
+ If your baby is still falling asleep at the breast or bottle most of the time it is a good idea to start to break this association by gently breaking the suction with your finger when she starts to get drowsy. You can then pat or rock her to sleep if you wish to.
+ Keep exposing your baby to filtered sunlight in the morning and between noon and 4 pm to help support the circadian system (see p. 7).
+ Continue to respond promptly to your baby's cries.
+ Some parents may want to occasionally give their baby opportunities to fall asleep on their own (see COTSS p. 90 for details).
+ Wrapping at this age may still help calm your baby until she falls asleep (see p. 13 on wrapping).
+ If your baby is still not showing tired signs after about two-and-a-half hours of being awake (including the time taken to feed), you may now consider winding her down to be ready for sleep.
+ It's okay to wake your baby if you think she is due for a feed.
+ A baby sling or carrier may be helpful for times your baby is unsettled and does not want to be put down. It is fine if she falls asleep in the sling sometimes.

Eight to Twelve Weeks

Routine

- Some parents find that getting themselves and their baby up at the same time each day is helpful in establishing a sense of order in their day.
- Go for a walk in the morning in the sunlight if possible and/or in the afternoon.
- Try feeding every three hours during the day.
- Make sure that night feeds are quiet, without talking or games, with the minimum attention given in the minimum of light.
- You can introduce a 'rollover feed' (also called a 'dream feed') at night (see p. 110 for explanation).
- Establish a sleep-time routine if you haven't already done so (see p. 90 for COTSS).

Day sleeps (napping)

DAY SLEEPS, OR NAPPING, ARE AN IMPORTANT PART OF BABIES' SLEEP HABITS AND ROUTINE

For the first month or so many babies sleep for most of the time,[3] it can seem as though all they do is eat and sleep. In these early weeks, it is often not necessary to get your baby to sleep, as most babies fall asleep wherever they are when they are tired. Sometimes the challenge is keeping your baby awake long enough to take a good feed!

Babies spend more and more time awake over the first couple of months, and start to play as well as feed and sleep.

Research shows that the earlier parents regulate the time of daytime sleeps (napping) in a baby the better for the development of routine.[24] A routine that is age appropriate and working well will usually result in your baby being sleepy at more or less the same time each day, and hungry at more or less the same time each day. This in turn makes the days more predictable and will make it very likely that your baby will be sleepy at the same time each night (thereby initiating a night-time routine). It is important to note here that it easier to find a routine to suit some babies (see Temperament and sleep, p. 25) but all babies benefit from a degree of routine in their day.

Day sleeps (napping) continued

HOW MUCH SLEEP DO BABIES NEED DURING THE DAY?

It can be hard for parents to know if their baby is getting enough daytime sleep. Recommended time spent asleep may be helpful (see Part 4 for this information), however it is important to note that every baby's sleep pattern differs, and some babies just do not need as much sleep as others. An important gauge as to whether a baby is getting enough sleep is whether or not she is happy for most of the time when she is awake. A baby that catnaps and is grumpy all the time may not be getting enough sleep. A baby who catnaps and wakes up happy and remains content for most of their awake time probably is getting enough sleep.

If your baby seems to be a catnapper, and you suspect he may not be getting enough sleep, you might like to try:

+ re-settling him with a minimum of fuss when he starts to stir awake (you may try patting, singing, wrapping or any other settling strategy that works for your baby)
+ going to your baby when he starts to stir awake (and is still drowsy) and transfer him to a carrier, pram or your arms to try to extend the sleep time in the short term. This may help to combine shorter naps into longer naps in their cot
+ encouraging quiet time, for example with some relaxing music at times during the day. Take the emphasis off sleep and onto relaxing for you both
+ using 'blackout' blinds or curtains in his room for day sleeps
+ getting your baby up for a short play or quiet activity such as reading together, and then try re-settling.

If all these fail you may have to get used to your catnapper for a while. Newborns look to a parent (usually the mother) to help regulate the pattern of day and night until they are more able to do this for themselves. Offer him more naps during the day (this sort of baby may continue to need four sleeps at a time that his peers are moving to three). Keep in mind that he may start to have longer day sleeps later in the first year when he is on the move and using more energy.

Eight to Twelve Weeks

Table 7: Baby sleep at a glance: eight to 12 weeks.

WHAT TO EXPECT	TIPS
Many babies are becoming accustomed to being in the world now, and are less distressed by simple events like bathing, nappy changes and tummy wind.	If your baby is still falling asleep at the breast or bottle, now is the time to gently discourage this by stopping the feed as she starts to get drowsy and then letting her continue to fall asleep on her own.
The amount of time your baby spends in active sleep (a lighter sleep) has reduced, and increasingly more time is spent in quiet sleep.	Getting your baby up and giving him the first feed at the same time each day can help establish a routine.
The circadian rhythm has started to develop, and so your baby's body and brain is starting to register the difference between night and day – this means the longest stretch of sleep in a 24-hour period should now be at night.	Try feeding every three hours during the day. This is a good length of time between feeds at this age to ensure your baby has a full feed while she's also getting used to having most of her feeds during the daytime hours.
Your baby may now be happily awake for about 3 hours during the day (including feeding time).	Now is the time to ensure that patterns of behaviour occur more consistently – for example feeding your baby when she wakes, then playing for a while and settling her to sleep without another feed will reduce the likelihood of feeding her to sleep becoming a problem.
Your baby will now probably be having 4 to 6 sleeps of 2 to 5 hours in length in a 24-hour period.	It's still fine for your baby to fall asleep (sometimes) in different places such as in the car, the pram or the sling.
	If your baby is not showing any tired signs after being awake for about two-and-a-half hours, you may want to start the process of getting her ready for sleep at that point.

See p. 90 for COTSS for this age.

Twelve to Sixteen Weeks

Development

Vision

Perception of detail improves greatly around this age, mainly due to development in the vision centres of the brain rather than the eye itself.

Thinking/feeling

Your baby's temperament is now becoming clearer. You may be feeling you now know what settles your baby – as well as what is likely to unsettle her.

A baby recognises repeated behaviour patterns but there is still no 'memory' stored at this age (see p. 63 for more information).

Behaviour and motor skills

+ Your baby's movements are becoming smoother as the brain develops and startle reflex starts to lessen around this time.
+ Your baby can now intentionally reach out, swipe at or perhaps even grab at things in his reach. Releasing his grasp on an object is much more difficult though!
+ Many babies are becoming more active and wanting more stimulation during their awake times.

Sleep

At this age, babies are often becoming more settled. The frequency and nature of night wakings may now be more predictable. If this isn't the case for you, don't worry; it does take longer for some babies to get into a routine.

+ The total sleep time in a 24-hour period is 15–17 hours on average.[23]
+ Babies may have two, three or four sleeps during the day.
+ At about this time 'active sleep' begins to mature to become REM sleep, and 'quiet sleep' becomes NREM sleep (see p. 6 for more on this)[23].
+ Babies have about 50 per cent of REM/active sleep (much more than adults). Because REM/active is a light sleep and is easy to wake from, your baby may still be waking frequently.
+ Most babies are now able to discern the difference between night and day, and are showing signs of adapting to this light–dark (day/night) cycle.
+ Babies may have five hours of straight sleep at night, followed by a feed, and another five hours.
+ Most babies are awake during the afternoon and early evening, though they may not be entirely happy at this time of day. In fact, many babies are unsettled at this time.
+ Your baby may now stay awake happily for two to three hours, and may be sleeping two hours at a time or longer during the day. Some babies may be catnapping through the day (see p. 101 on napping).

 *Sleeping for the whole night is the exception rather than the rule. Researchers who study babies who 'sleep through the night' actually consider a 5–6 hour stretch at night as 'sleeping through'.*[23]

What to expect

+ Because breast milk is digested more easily than formula, breast-fed babies are more likely than bottle-fed babies to wake more frequently for a feed at night. This is normal and not a sign that your baby has a sleep problem.
+ Self-soothing behaviours, i.e. the ability to sleep or calm down after an upset (without help), are still only seen occasionally at this age and even if they are evident, your baby may not be able to consistently use them.
+ Signs of tiredness begin to change from the newborn signs. Look for loss of interest in toys or playing, fretting, yawning, crying or eye rubbing; or a change in level of physical activity (either less or more).

Practical tips

+ It is reasonable to now start limit setting around feeding, and actively discouraging your baby from falling asleep at the breast or bottle. If your baby tends to fall asleep when feeding, gently break the suction (and stop the feed) when he starts to get drowsy. You can then rock and pat him to sleep or wrap and/or give him a dummy. Aim to feed your baby upon waking, not when he is due for a sleep. This will minimise the likelihood of your baby falling asleep while feeding and developing this sleep association (see p. 9 for sleep associations).
+ If you haven't already done so, you should now start to establish a consistent, predictable and soothing bedtime routine and ritual. (See p. 111 for example.)
+ A great way to start to establish a routine is to get your baby up and fed at the same time each morning.
+ You can now start to wait a little before attending to your baby if you feel she is not upset or distressed (see p. 112 for how to tell if your baby is distressed). You don't need to jump to attention the instant she cries any more, but try calling from another room that you are coming in a minute, or let her wait for a minute or two.

- As the startle reflexes evident at birth have often reduced by now, it may be possible to adjust your wrapping technique slightly, with a view to stopping wrapping if you wish to. (See p. 13 for more tips on how to prepare for no more wrapping.) It is fine to keep wrapping your baby if you want to, but you will need a bigger wrap, or a specialised wrap, to prevent him coming free of the wrapping and needing to be re-wrapped to resettle.
- It is important to consider sleep associations as they are easily established at this age. Reducing or avoiding sleep associations that you don't want (feeding to sleep, etc.) is becoming increasingly important from this stage onward (see p. 12 for sleep associations).
- Aim for most of your baby's sleeps to now be in her own bed, although it is still okay to have a catnap late in the day in the car, pram or baby sling.
- Any routine established will stay more or less the same for a couple of months. The actual times may change a bit (your baby may not be ready for sleep until later in the morning) but the general order of events has become increasingly predictable for most families.

It is natural and important for a baby to experience all the negative emotions: fear, sorrow, frustration; but essential too that they are not left feeling that way for too long.[25]

At this age, allowing your baby to wait a short time for you (when she is somewhere between totally happy and unhappy) encourages the development of self-soothing behaviours. It also teaches you about your child's limits and capacity to wait and teaches you something about your own capacity to tolerate your baby's protesting and complaining.

Twelve to Sixteen Weeks

Routine

What might a normal day be like? Many parents find it helpful to start the day at about the same time and have bedtime for the baby at about the same time as well. Remember to try to feed your baby three to four hourly during the day.

Table 8: A possible daily routine at 12 to 16 weeks.

TIME	ACTIVITY
7 am	Feed and stay awake for about an hour
8–9 am	Sleep for an hour or two
10 am	Feed and stay awake for an hour or two
Middle of the day	Sleep for an hour or two
2–3 pm	Feed and awake for an hour or two
Some babies may need a late afternoon nap. Those who don't sleep may well be grumpy in the late afternoon/early evening. It is still fine for this afternoon nap to be in a sling, or in the car or pram if you are out and about.	
5.30–6 pm	Feed
	Bath or wash and ready for bed
	Top-up feed
7–8 pm	COTSS and into their own bed
10–11 pm	Rollover feed if you are doing this
	Use the COTSS techniques for getting baby back to sleep (see p. 111)
An overnight feed (or two) is still very common at this age.	

Remember not all babies are created equal! Not all babies will be easy to settle at this age, and not all will be moving into an established routine. Even with a more-difficult-to-settle baby, you can use the strategies described here. The same rules apply but the baby might take longer to settle into a routine.

The challenge is to keep carrying out these settling techniques, even if there is no apparent benefit yet. Be patient, the benefit will come in time, some babies just take a little longer than others.

What is a 'rollover' feed?
(OTHERWISE REFERRED TO AS A 'DREAM FEED')

A rollover, or dream feed, is a feed that is given last thing at night to a half-asleep baby.

To give a rollover feed, gently rouse your sleeping baby enough that she will take a feed, but not enough to give her the message it is time to fully wake up.

The rollover feed is given in the same way as a night feed, with minimum attention and fuss, and with dimmed lights and no talking. The time of the rollover feed is somewhere between 9.30 and 11.30 pm.

A rollover feed works well for some babies, but not all. It doesn't work well when the baby doesn't wake enough to take a full feed (so there's no point!), or when he wakes too much (and thinks it's playtime). Some babies take a full feed peacefully, but then wake anyway for another feed during the night. If this is the case for you, it may be worth trying again in a few weeks.

The COTSS Method (Creating Opportunities To Self-Soothe) for three to ten months

The following steps show you how to give your baby the opportunity to learn self-soothing skills around sleep time.

1. Start slowing and calming your activity around your baby as sleep time approaches.
2. Check that your baby's needs have been take care of (clean nappy, fed, burped, etc.).
3. Take your baby to his sleep room.
4. Read a book together, sing a bedtime song.
5. Wrap (if you are using a wrap).
6. Give him his sleep aid (such as a dummy or cuddle toy after six months).
7. Cuddle your baby in your arms, rock/sway/pat gently until he is very calm. Relaxing lullaby music can be part of this ritual if you like.
8. Say, 'Ssh – it's sleep time,' or whatever else you like (a short lullaby for example).
9. Put your baby down in his cot. Activate the lullaby toy if he has one.
10. Leave your baby to see if he can settle to sleep on his own. Notice what he does as he gets ready for sleep. Is he showing signs of self-soothing?
11. If he cries go to him and pat or rub his back for a couple of minutes.

Repeat your sleep words or song. Listen and watch – is he calming down? Sometimes babies make a repetitive noise as they are winding down for sleep.

If the crying escalates and he sounds as though he is getting distressed, repeat steps 7 to 10.

You can repeat these as many times as you like until your baby settles to sleep, but if it does not seem to be working let your baby fall asleep however he can and try again in a couple of days or weeks.

The COTSS method suggests:

+ you place your baby into her bed while awake but drowsy. Some babies adjust to this easier than others (see temperament p. 25) so if at first you don't succeed, try again in a few weeks
+ if your baby is falling asleep while sucking at the breast/bottle or dummy, you can try removing the nipple/teat gently by breaking the suction with your little finger and seeing if she can continue to fall asleep on her own without the sucking
+ you do *not* leave your baby to cry in distress.

How do you know if your baby is distressed?

Signs to look out for are sobbing, sweating, screaming, a racing heart, a red face and a frantic look. When babies feel like this, it is very difficult for them to calm themselves down, and virtually impossible for them to fall asleep without help because of the physiological arousal occurring in their body.

The Sensible Sleep Solution does not recommend leaving your baby cry to distress.

Twelve to Sixteen Weeks

Table 9: Baby sleep at a glance: 12 to 16 weeks.

WHAT TO EXPECT	TIPS
Many babies are becoming accustomed to being in the world, and are less distressed by simple events like bathing, nappy changes and tummy wind. Your baby's sleep pattern is maturing, and babies spend less time in active sleep, and more time in quiet sleep. The circadian rhythm is continuing to develop so that most babies are naturally having their longest stretch of sleep at night. Your baby may be happily awake for about 3 hours during the day (including feeding time). Your baby will probably be having 3 to 5 sleeps of 2 to 5 hours in length in a 24-hour period. Signs of tiredness may change from those of the newborn stage. Tired signs to look for now are crying, irritability, loss of interest in toys, avoiding eye contact, yawning and eye rubbing.	If your baby is still falling asleep at the breast or bottle, now is the time to gently start to stop this by stopping the feed as she starts to get drowsy and then letting her continue to fall asleep on her own. Getting your baby up and giving him the first feed at the same time each day can help in the establishment of a routine. Try feeding every 3 hours during the day. For many babies of this age a 3-hour break ensures they are having a full feed while also getting most of their feeds in during the daytime hours. Now is the time to ensure that predictable patterns of behaviour occur more consistently – for example feeding your baby when he wakes up, then playing for a while and settling to sleep without another feed will reduce the likelihood of feeding to sleep becoming a problem. It's still fine for your baby to fall asleep in different places, such as in the car, the pram or the sling, however, depending on your baby's temperament, some babies will sleep better in their own bed. If your baby is not showing any tired signs after being awake for about 2½ to 3 hours, you may want to start the process of getting her ready for her sleep at that point. Now is the time to establish a consistent, calm bedtime ritual if you have not already. An example of a night-time bedtime routine is bath, feed, story, song and bed. Some babies will respond well to having a rollover feed (see p. 110) between 10 and 11 pm.

Four to Six Months

Development

Vision

By now most babies will be able to predict (not just follow) with their eyes the position of a steadily moving object. It is now clear that your baby is *choosing* to look at certain things, rather than being compelled to. Babies are able to change their gaze easily and willingly.

Hearing

Most babies are able to distinguish the full range of frequencies and locate sounds, but their hearing has not yet reached full maturity and they are still a little hard of hearing. They can recognise voices and locate where they are coming from more easily than when younger.

Thinking/feeling

Many babies are now beginning to regulate their cortisol levels (see p. 35). This means they are not as easily distressed as in the earlier months, more able to tolerate some frustration, and more able to calm themselves down after an upset.

Whilst babies are now able to identify behavioural patterns (what happens next when something familiar happens), memory is held for only a few days to a week at a time, and only when prompted.

Your baby's dislikes, likes and preferences are becoming more evident as their personality emerges more strongly.

Behaviour and motor skills

+ Self-soothing behaviours become more common from this age, with your baby's increased capacity for regulating the stress hormone cortisol.

- Most babies are now mouthing objects to find out more about them (putting things like their hands and toys in their mouth).
- By six months of age a baby can:
  - hold her head erect
  - push up on her forearms when on her tummy
  - reach and grab for toys
  - roll over (but her arm may get trapped underneath her)
  - take an increasing interest in the world around her and is distracted by sights and sounds during feeding time during the day
  - produce a range of consonants. B, D, M, N, W and Y are early sounds and can now be produced in repetitive syllables as babbling, e.g. babababa, mamamama, dadadada. This is a due to brain development as well as the development of the throat, mouth and tongue.

Sleep

- Total time spent asleep averages 14–17 hours per day.[23]
- Babies' sleep patterns are becoming more predictable.
- 'Active sleep' is the sleep onset stage; this means that babies are still jerky and twitching and easily disturbed while they are falling asleep.[3] This explains why, if your baby falls asleep in your arms, he may jerk awake when you move to place him in his bed.
- Babies have now adapted to the light/dark cycle and now 'know' the difference between day and night.
- Many babies will now be having two to three daytime naps, and the longest sleep period will be at night. Some babies may be having short more frequent catnaps (three to four sleeps during the day). This may be annoying for you but it's fine for your baby. The total hours spent asleep in a 24-hour period is just as important as how many sleeps they have.

Four to Six Months

What to expect
- Some babies start on solids between four and six months of age. Seek your health professional's advice on whether or not your baby is ready for solids.
- There is steady progress in your baby's ability to communicate her needs with you in ways other than crying so you may find it is getting easier (most of the time!) to understand your baby's needs and wants.

Practical tips
- If your baby is sleeping in a cot in your room, now is good time to move the cot (and the baby!) to the place that you ultimately want him sleeping (such as his own room or a sibling's room).
- A transitional object (soothing toy or piece of fabric, see p. 121 for more information) can be introduced ready for a surge in attachment behaviours at around the six-month mark.
- If you haven't already, now is a good time to introduce games and activities that help your baby begin to understand that even though she can't see you, you have not disappeared. Examples of such games or activities are peek-a-boo, and talking to your baby from behind a cloth or from another room.
- If you have not already established a consistent, predictable and soothing bedtime routine, now is the time to do it. Use COTSS for this age (see p. 111).
- Trying different ways to settle your baby into a calm and sleepy state (rocking, walking, patting, singing, sitting) reduces the likelihood of him becoming dependent on one method for calming or settling down (see p. 33 for ideas of calming strategies).
- If you haven't already, consider introducing a rollover feed (at about 10–11 pm) to encourage a long sleep through the night. (See p. 110 for more information on rollover feeds.)

Four to Six Months

Table 10: A possible daily routine at four to six months.

TIME	ACTIVITY
7 am	Feed and stay awake for about 2 hours
9 am	Settle to sleep
10–11 am	Feed on waking and then playtime for about 2 hours
Noon	Settle to sleep
1–2 pm	Feed on waking and then playtime for about 2 hours
3 pm	Settle to sleep
4–5 pm	Feed on waking and then playtime or spend time in sling
6–8 pm	Bath or wash and prepare for bed. Top-up feed COTSS
9.30–11.30 pm	Rollover feed if you are doing one

It is still very normal for a baby of this age to wake for an overnight feed (or even two!).

Of course, your routine may be different than this example. See your health professional (GP, early childhood nurse) if you would like help developing a routine that suits you and your family's circumstances.

Tips for developing a routine

+ Start each day at more or less the same time (i.e. get yourself and your baby up at the same time each day).
+ Throughout the day feed your baby when she wakes.
+ Space feeds *at least* two-and-a-half hours, but not more than four hours apart during the day.
+ Settle your baby to sleep when you see tired signs.
+ Ensure night feeds are quiet and as low fuss as possible.

Case study

In the first few weeks I was happy to just completely follow Indy's lead. At times she slept pretty well at night, when she was about nine weeks old she slept from 8.30 pm until 4 am! I woke up in a panic, but that's another story.

Anyway, up until now I haven't been bothered about what times she sleeps and feeds and have hardly even known what day it is let alone what time. But now I'm starting to want to get out and about more and would really like a bit of routine in my day. I decided a few days ago to start getting myself and Indy up at the same time each morning and then trying to feed at more or less the same time each day.

It seems to be working okay for us. We'll see how it goes, but I do feel more in charge of the day now.

Sarah, mother of Indica, 4 months

our thoughts

Generally speaking, the older a baby gets the easier it becomes to settle her, and for her to settle herself. But remember, not all babies are created equal!

Predictability and consistency is comforting to all babies, but some at this age can still be hard to settle, hard to read, and unable to self-soothe.

The parental challenge is to keep persisting with routine, consistency and predictability, even if you cannot see the benefit at first.

Four to Six Months

Case study

Oscar's routine (6½ months)

6–6.30 am	*Breakfast (cereal and fruit)*
8–8.30 am	*Milk (150–200 ml) then sleep*
10.30–11 am	*Lunch (vegetables or fruit and yoghurt)*
12.30–1.30 pm	*Milk (150–200 ml) then sleep*
5 pm	*Dinner (vegetables then yoghurt and/or fruit)*
6 pm (ish)	*Bath with Toby*
6.30 pm	*Milk (150–200 ml) then bed*

Oscar will wake once or twice during the night for milk, and then settle back to sleep. I put him in a sleeping bag, cuddle and kiss him, then tell him, 'It's time for a sleep,' put him in cot with dummies and leave. He'll whinge and talk for about five minutes and then usually put himself to sleep.

He may wake after 40 to 45 minutes and probably just needs me to locate a dummy for him so he can go back to sleep or he may just have had enough sleep! I give him a dummy and leave him for five to ten minutes to see if he goes back to sleep.

And I only go back in to him if he really loses it or cries for more than a few minutes.

Tara, mother of Oscar and Toby

Transitional objects

A transitional object is an object that soothes and comforts a baby or child, and 'reminds' the baby or child of the comfort that they get from their main caregiver. Transitional objects are very helpful for supporting the development of self-soothing behaviours.

Transitional objects are generally soft toys or a piece of material such as a special blanket or handkerchief. Transitional objects can be introduced at any time from about 4 months of age. Introducing a transitional object involves having the toy or cloth as part of the soothing and relaxing time between you and your baby. For example, you could ensure that the toy was part of story and feed time before bed by always having the toy with you at these times and even gently encouraging your baby to hold or touch the toy as they read the story or feed. Remember that the object will not immediately be comforting so don't offer it when your baby is upset and expect your baby to calm down. It is not the object in itself that will eventually help you baby self-soothe, it is the association between the object and you and calm feelings. This develops over time.

(Remember that soft toys and other transitional objects should not be left in the cot with your baby for the first 12 months.)

Four to Six Months

Table 11: Baby sleep at a glance: four to six months.

WHAT TO EXPECT	TIPS
Self-soothing behaviours become more common at this age, and many babies are getting better at calming down after an upset.	Watch your baby after an upset – what does he do to try and calm himself down?
Your baby's likes and dislikes and his temperament are becoming easier to read.	If your baby is still sleeping in your room and this is not where you want him to stay, now is a good time to move him to his own room.
Many babies start to show more predictability in the times of day that they are hungry, tired etc., making your day more predictable and manageable.	Keep following a predictable bedtime routine or ritual each night at sleep time. This helps your baby prepare for sleep.
Most babies will now be having 2 to 3 daytime naps, and the longest sleep will be at night.	Ensure that predictable patterns of behaviour occur consistently – for example feeding your baby when he wakes, then playing for a while and settling to sleep without another feed will reduce the likelihood of feeding to sleep becoming a problem.
It is still normal for babies to wake for a feed overnight.	
Your baby may now be happily awake for about 3 hours during the day (including feeding time).	It's still fine for your baby to fall asleep sometimes in different places, such as in the car, the pram or the sling. Some babies prefer to sleep in their own bed.

See p. 111 for COTSS for this age.

Six to Eight Months

Development

Thinking/feeling

- This is the age for a leap in development of the part of the brain responsible for emotional attachment. You may see the emergence of 'separation anxiety', which means your baby feels uneasy when not with the person or people she loves best.
- Babies can now remember a behaviour pattern, as well as predict what will happen next from past experience (provided this past experience has been repeated a number of times and is not more than a few days ago!).
- Your baby's ability to regulate cortisol (the stress hormone) continues to steadily improve.

Behaviour and motor skills

- Hand–eye coordination has improved so your baby can more easily hold things, like toys or rattles. Some babies may be able to pass objects from one hand to another, though many find it difficult to release objects from their grasp.
- Babies can grab their feet when lying on their back, and may even enjoy putting their feet in their mouth.
- Some babies will start to sit, aided or not, during this time. This allows your baby more opportunity to look around.
- Babies may become clingier to their main carer or carers. Researchers think that attachment behaviours like 'clinginess' increase at this time so the baby will stay close to his mum and therefore safe, even though he can now move away.
- Babies may begin to protest at being left alone in a room, and may have difficulty going to sleep alone (even those babies who have slept well in their own bed up until now). Your baby's clinging behaviours and protesting at being left alone are still instinctual (designed to keep you close by and her safe) and not intentional to trick or manipulate you. Attachment needs are real needs (see p. 53 for more

Six to Eight Months

information on attachment. See COTSS for this age on how to manage this at sleep time, p. 111).
- Many babies can now roll in both directions (from front to back and back to front).
- Babies may now be able to move to satisfy their need for repetitive motion such as bouncing, swaying, body rocking or in some cases, head banging[13] (see p. 127).
- Because your baby is beginning to remember things, they recognise (and prefer) familiar people. The flip side of this is that they are also aware of who is *not* familiar and may respond by showing stranger anxiety.

Sleep

- Most babies will now be having two or three sleeps during the day and longer stretches at night.
- Total sleep time averages 14–16 hours per day.[23]
- Sleep cycles now more closely resemble the older child and adult pattern of REM and non-REM sleep.[3] Active or REM sleep now has reduced to about 30 to 40 per cent of sleep time.
- There is now the brain maturity for your baby to settle into a longer period of sleep, perhaps up to eight to ten hours per night if you are lucky!
- Many health professionals say that babies who are at least six months of age and growing well do not need a feed during the night (meaning five or six hours of uninterrupted sleep). So now is the time to start reducing night feeds if you want to do this (see p. 130 for tips on how to do this).
- Your baby may be calling you more through the night, even if she had previously slept quite well. Given the surge in attachment behaviour, it is just as likely to be a need for reconnection and closeness as it is for a feed. Also, many babies are starting to practise new skills at this age, such as rolling or even crawling, and may start to practise in the middle of the night, thus unsettling and disturbing themselves and their parents!

What to expect

+ Only about 50 per cent of babies self-soothe at this age. This means that many cannot self-soothe and therefore still need someone to help them calm down after an upset.[7]
+ At six months of age, 50 to 75 per cent of babies are sleeping for a five-hour stretch at night.[23]
+ Remember that even babies who were sleeping well when younger may start waking more for reasons such as increased motor activity and attachment-seeking behaviours – or they may be teething.

Parental challenges

+ Night waking in babies who were previously sleeping well can be frustrating and exasperating for parents. It is important to remember that night waking at this age is normal, and not a sign of anything wrong.
+ Reducing overnight feeding can be a challenge (see box p. 130).
+ Some parents feel a sense of sadness or loss when their baby no longer needs a feed in the middle of the night. They may have enjoyed the peacefulness and connection of this night feed (particularly if the day is very busy or taken up with other things and people) and feel a loss when it goes.
+ Your baby may become more 'clingy' at this time (coinciding with a surge in development and attachment). This may be a challenge for some parents.
+ Telling what, if anything, your baby needs at this age can be a challenge. There may be a myriad of questions. Does he still *need* a night feed or not? Is she teething? Has she got sore legs from trying to crawl? Does his tummy ache from that new food he ate today? Is he sensitive or allergic to the new food? Perhaps he is hungry? Does he still need to be wrapped? Should I still be going to him in the night?

Six to Eight Months

Head banging

HEAD BANGING IN THE SECOND HALF OF THE FIRST YEAR IS SOMETIMES USED BY BABIES AS A MEANS OF SELF-SOOTHING.[23]

Body rocking and head banging are usually normal behaviours in babies, who seem to find the rhythmic rocking backwards and forwards comforting, and an aid to falling asleep. Body rocking often starts at about six months of age and a few months later may be accompanied by head banging or head rolling. Some babies rock backwards and forwards on all fours, others rock while sitting up.

Body rocking and/or head banging are not usually an indication of anything wrong when seen in otherwise healthy children at sleep time. Babies usually grow out of this, but some adults still use body rocking as a way of self-soothing. In some cases head banging can indicate pain in the head or ear, so it is worthwhile having a GP check your baby's ears for signs of fluid or infection.

If you are concerned about your baby's body rocking or head banging seek medical advice.

Practical tips

+ A consistent, predictable and soothing bedtime routine is very important at this age. Your baby can now follow repeated patterns of behaviour and is also starting to be able to predict behaviour patterns. Babies of this age increasingly need the security that comes with predictability.
+ At this time it is reasonable to get rid of any night feeds between midnight and 5 am. A rollover feed between 9.30 and 11.30 pm (see p. 110) may help your baby last through to 5 or 6 am without another feed. (See p. 130 for how to reduce night feeding.)
+ You may consider a dim nightlight to allow your baby to orientate himself when he wakes at night.
+ Most babies at this age sleep best at bedtime if they are awake from their day sleep by 3 to 3.30 pm.

Six to Eight Months

- Your baby calling at night is not always about the need to be fed. As it is a time of attachment surge and separation anxiety it is possible that your baby feels a need for this connection in the middle of the night, rather than the feed. The use of a transitional object may provide some comfort to your baby when you are not around. (See p. 121 for how to use and introduce a transitional comfort toy.)
- Going into your baby at night is still important. Going in will help *you* learn what your baby is calling for. In time you will be able to trust your own knowledge about what your baby needs (or does not need), so you will not need to rely on others' words of wisdom about how you should be responding to your baby in the middle of the night. You can learn this for yourself.

our thoughts

Research shows that babies over six months of age can, on average, sleep through the night without the need for a night feed[23] – 'through the night' still means five or six hours though! Some points to consider:
- Not all babies are average. Weight as well as age needs to be considered when deciding if your baby does not need a feed during the night. Check with your early childhood nurse or GP about how your baby is developing if you are thinking of dropping the night feed.
- Remember your baby needs enough calories in the day to be able to drop his night feed.
- Remember that breast milk is digested faster than formula, so a breast-fed baby may still require a feed in the night – this is still considered normal and not a sleep or feeding problem.

Six to Eight Months

Table 12: A possible daily routine at six to eight months.

TIME	ACTIVITY
7 am	Milk feed on waking
	Breakfast (solids)
	Playtime/awake time for about 2 hours
9 am	Settle to sleep
11 am	Milk feed on waking
	Playtime/awake time
Noon	Lunch (solids)
	Playtime/awake time
1–2 pm	Settle to sleep
4 pm	Milk feed on waking
	Playtime/awake time
5 pm	Dinner (solids)
	Playtime/awake time
	Bath time
7 pm	Milk feed
	Settle to sleep (COTSS)
9.30–11.30 pm	Rollover feed if you are doing one

It is still normal for a baby of this age to wake for an overnight feed (see below for tips on reducing night feeds if you wish to try these).

(Remember, this is an example only, and your routine must suit your circumstances. See p. 66 for tips on developing a routine.)

 Tips for reducing night feeds

There is no magic answer to this tricky situation, but these tips may be helpful.

BREASTFEEDING

+ Reduce the time spent feeding by two to five minutes each night, over a week – or two or three.
+ Offer a bottle of water and a short cuddle instead of a breastfeed.
+ Introduce a rollover feed (see p. 110).

BOTTLE-FEEDING

+ Reduce the amount of milk given at the feed by 5–10 ml a night, over a week – or two or three.
+ Offer a bottle of water and a short cuddle instead of a feed.
+ Introduce a rollover feed.

Six to Eight Months

Table 13: Baby sleep at a glance: six to eight months.

WHAT TO EXPECT	TIPS
There is a leap in development of the area of the brain responsible for emotional attachment, and it is normal for babies to become clingier to their parents.	Watch your baby after an upset – what does he do to try and calm himself down?
Many babies show a strong preference for being with their main carer, and may be reluctant to go to others or to be left alone in a room.	It is important to bear in mind that any increase in clingy behaviour, and/or protesting at being left are normal attachment behaviours of this age.
There may be an increase in calling behaviours at night, even for babies who have been sleeping well at night.	If possible, reassure your baby by ensuring that she is not left to the point of becoming distressed.
Many babies start to show more predictability in the times of day that they are hungry, tired etc., making your day more predictable and manageable.	Keep following a predictable bedtime routine or ritual each night at sleep time. This helps your baby prepare for sleep. A regular bed time is becoming increasingly important for the establishment of a routine.
Most babies will now be having 2 to 3 daytime naps, and the longest sleep will be at night.	Ensure that predictable patterns of behaviour occur consistently – for example feeding your baby when he wakes, then playing and settling to sleep without another feed will reduce the likelihood of feeding to sleep becoming a problem.
It is still quite normal for breastfed babies to wake for a feed overnight. See opposite page for how to reduce night feeding if you want to do this.	Consider using a night-light and introducing some comforting objects (see p. 121 to support self-soothing at night).

See p. 111 for COTSS for this age.

Eight to Ten Months

Development
Thinking/feeling
- There are enormous changes and growth in brain function at this age,[18] particularly in the frontal lobes (see brain development p. 58). This is the part of the brain that is involved in thinking, self-control and regulating emotion. This means that babies are starting to make sense of their emotions and relate them to what is going on around them and then putting this knowledge to use.
- For the first time babies can intentionally come up with a plan of action and follow it through, e.g. she will drop a toy in anticipation of you picking it up for her.
- At this point *recall* memory starts to emerge. Recall memory is basically the brain's ability to call up an image in one's mind, without any prompt being necessary. So your baby can now think of you even when you are not there.

Behaviour and motor skills
- Your baby might now be crawling or moving around on his own in some other way. This means that you may have to start setting limits around safety, and ensure that your home is 'babyproof'.
- Babies are beginning to be aware of others' emotions and may interact in ways that show this (for example offering objects or food to others, and pointing to something interesting to share it with others).
- Your baby may now sit without support and some will be pulling themselves up to stand.
- Babies are now enjoying imitating others' sounds and actions.
- Many babies can grasp small items with their thumb and forefinger (the 'pincer' grasp).

Babies at this age can increasingly plan their behaviour. An experiment demonstrated this planning and regulation of behaviour. At eight months of age a baby faced with a Lego block placed in a clear open-topped box cannot stop themselves from trying to get to the block straight through the plastic side (repeatedly hitting their hand on the side). At nine months, they work out that they can get the block from over the top of the plastic most of the time (can plan new behaviours and then do them most of the time). At 11 months of age babies get the block from over the top of the plastic every time. This demonstrates the development of self-control of thoughts and actions.[18]

Sleep

+ REM/active sleep accounts for about 30–40 per cent of total sleep.[23]
+ Many babies are now having two daytime sleeps and the rest of their sleep at night. Catnappers may still be having three shorter sleeps.
+ Total sleep time averages 13–16 hours per 24-hour day.[23]
+ From about nine months of age, babies appear to dream, or to be affected by dreaming.
+ The new skills, feelings and experiences associated with a surge in brain development at this age may feel a little overwhelming for some babies, and they may need extra reassurance and so call for a parent's attention during the night (even if they were sleeping well in earlier months).
+ About 50 per cent of babies can now self-soothe, and about 70–80 per cent sleep for a five or six-hour stretch between midnight and 5 am at nine months.[26]

Eight to Ten Months

What to expect

+ Babies may show more persistence in getting what they want. This is because your baby can now remember behaviour patterns and have preferences (and can remember what they are!).
+ You may have a clearer idea why your baby is waking and calling for attention at night, and so you feel more confident about making informed decisions about how to respond.
+ Some babies can now stand up in their cot, which may present a problem when getting them to sleep. Babies who want to practise standing up by pulling themselves up on the cot, may not be able (or may not feel confident) to get back down again. See box for tips on what to do about this.

Tips for dealing with cot standing

The important thing for your baby to learn once she can stand herself up in the cot is *how to get back down*. When you go in to your baby encourage her to get herself back down with a minimum of fuss and attention. Gently slide her hands down the rails of the cot until she is seated, telling her clearly, 'It's time for sleep now.' Let her practise this skill during the day as well. Remember, it will take some time for your baby to learn this, and to feel confident doing it without help.

Parental challenges

+ This can be a challenging time for parents. Babies have *some* capacity to regulate their emotions, *some* control over their behaviour and also a surge in brain development and ability to move which means they may also be experiencing separation anxiety.[27] They will also be trying new foods and perhaps teething, which makes it very difficult for parents to know what their baby's needs and wants are, and to work out how to respond. This comes at a time when many parents thought that they would be finally getting a full night's sleep!
+ Some babies still only catnap during the day. You can still develop a routine around a catnapper, but it's challenging for parents who may still feel at the mercy of their baby's daytime sleep (see p. 101 for more information on day time naps).
+ Your baby is now becoming more able to tolerate some bedtime and night-time limit setting, because they are now beginning to understand cause and effect. This does not mean that they will always like the limits that parents set; it is part of the normal run of things for a baby to react against these limits at times by crying, appearing frustrated or even angry. This behaviour is normal, but it may be a challenge for parents who find strong emotions difficult to bear.
+ Moving into a new way of parenting that includes limit setting is a real challenge for parents of babies at this age. It is not necessary to set limits for a baby who lies in the one spot, but is for a baby who moves around and is starting to test how the world works and what will get a reaction from parents and what will not.
+ Parents can find themselves disagreeing for the first time about what are reasonable limits to set for their baby: to what extent do we babyproof our house? When should we say 'no' to our baby? How will limit setting be handled? Talk about it. Do you and your partner/family agree on how to handle your baby's reaction to limit setting?

Eight to Ten Months

Table 14: A possible daily routine at eight to ten months.

TIME	ACTIVITY
7 am	Milk feed on waking Breakfast (solids) Playtime/awake time for about 2 hours
9 am	Settle to sleep
11 am	Milk feed on waking Playtime/awake time
Noon	Lunch (solids) Playtime/awake time
2 pm	Settle to sleep
4 pm	Milk feed on waking Playtime/awake time
5 pm	Dinner (solids) Playtime/awake time Bath time
7 pm	Milk feed (may be from a bottle, cup or breast) Settle to sleep (COTSS)
9.30–11.30 pm	Rollover feed if you are doing one

Babies may still be waking in the night for a feed. See p. 130 for tips on how to reduce these if you would like to.

(Remember, this is an example only, and your routine must suit your circumstances. See p. 118 for tips on developing a routine.)

Eight to Ten Months

Setting limits around sleep time for eight to 12-month-old babies

Parents who have prepared their babies and themselves throughout most of the first year with creating opportunities to self-soothe, and with some basic limits setting, can now confidently extend these limits to bedtime and night-time, knowing that this is an appropriate age to do so because their baby:

+ can understand what is expected of him
+ is starting to be able to control his behaviour
+ has some capacity for soothing and calming himself down (this may be with the aid of a comfort toy or sleep aid of some sort).

Protesting about going to bed and sleep is normal at this age and there may be some indignant crying. This is normal and to be expected. Your baby is just communicating his disapproval!

Now is the time to draw on all the knowledge you have learned from your experiences over the past eight to 12 months to answer this question: does my baby really have a need that must be met, or is he protesting about these limits I am now setting? Listen to what the cry sounds like. If the crying escalates to a distressed cry, go to the baby, even if it has only been one minute since you last attended to him.

When you start setting limits, your baby may protest. It is important to watch (or rather listen) to your baby, not the clock. There is no magic technique needed and no magic number of minutes to wait until you attend to him.

our thoughts

Limit setting in practice – some things are not negotiable!

Some babies object to being put in their car seat at this age. They cry in protest and seem unhappy and frustrated. This can be hard to hear, and uncomfortable to bear. But it would be unheard of for a parent to then say, 'Oh well, you can just stand up in the car then while we go for a drive.' Because of the real concerns about safety, parents persist and find a way to get their baby safely into their car seat, despite the crying and protesting and frustration, because they know what is best for their baby, and their baby does not have the capacity or information to know what is best for them.

This is the same type of crying that happens when limits are set around other matters that are important for your baby's safety and well-being, such as limit setting around going to bed, staying in bed, having a hair wash or being strapped in a high chair. Remember that babies may cry and protest when limits are set for them, and this is normal.

Eight to Ten Months

When you do go in to him, there is absolutely no need to avoid eye contact or be any different than usual; just be yourself and give the consistent and clear message: 'You are fine where you are and it's now time for sleep.'

Note: If you think that there is need for a quick cuddle, it's fine to do this to reassure yourself and your baby that everything is all right in the world and between you. If you want to pick your baby up for a cuddle, do so. If you prefer to comfort him while he is still in his cot, that's fine too. The message is always the same: 'I'm here, you're okay in your bed and it's now time for sleep.' The Sensible Sleep Solution says that you can take care of your baby's needs but do not have to pander to his wants (which may be 'rock me to sleep please').

The COTSS Method (Creating Opportunities To Self-Soothe) for eight to twelve months

The following steps show you how to give your baby the opportunity to use some self-soothing skills around sleep time.

1. Start slowing and calming your activity around your baby as sleep time approaches.
2. Check that your baby's needs have been take care of (clean nappy, fed, burped, etc.).
3. Take your baby to her sleep room.
4. Read a book together, sing a bedtime song.
5. Wrap her (if you are still using a wrap).
6. Give your baby her sleep aid (such as a dummy or cuddle toy).
7. Cuddle her in your arms, rock/sway/pat gently until she is relaxed. Relaxing lullaby music can be part of this ritual if you like.
8. Say, 'Ssh – it's sleep time,' or whatever else you like that sends the message that it is now sleep time (a short lullaby about sleep or closing eyes for example).
9. Put your baby down in the cot, activate her lullaby toy if she has one, and say goodnight. You can stay in the room sitting quietly in a chair or leave the room; it's up to you to decide what is best for you and your baby.
10. If your baby cries with distress go to her, look at her and say, 'It's time for sleep now,' or similar and then leave her to settle down.

If the crying escalates and she sounds as though she is getting distressed, repeat steps 7 to 10. You can even go back to step 4 if she gets cross and frustrated at being in your arms.

Try not to leave your baby until she becomes *distressed*, as it will then take longer for her to calm down and be ready for sleep. If the crying is escalating (getting louder and more insistent) go and check what her needs are and take care of these, then leave her to the business of falling asleep. The trick is to avoid letting her get distressed, to go in before this time to take care of any needs, and allow her to then settle to sleep. Through your consistent behaviour at bedtime your baby will come to understand two things:

+ you are consistently there to take care of her needs
+ you have clear expectations of what happens around sleep time, and your behaviour is predictable.

Note that the Sensible Sleep Solution, which uses the COTSS techniques for calming and settling, does not recommend leaving a baby to cry in distress.

our thoughts

Signs of distress in a baby include sobbing, sweating, screaming, a racing heart, a red face and a 'frantic' look. It is very difficult for babies to calm themselves enough to fall asleep when they are very distressed.

Eight to Ten Months

Table 15: Baby sleep at a glance: eight to ten months.

WHAT TO EXPECT	TIPS
At this time there is a leap in development of the area of the brain responsible for self control and emotional regulation. This means that babies are starting to understand cause and effect. Many babies are now starting to move around on their own, or be practising doing so. Some babies are pulling to stand. This may mean that babies are practising these skills when they are in their bed at night. There may be an increase in calling behaviours at night, even for babies who have been sleeping well at night. Most babies will now be having 2 to 3 daytime naps at predictable times during the day, and the longest period will be at night.	Watch your baby after an upset – what does he do to try and calm himself down? Some limit setting is becoming important as your baby starts to understand cause and effect and starts testing certain kinds of behaviour to see what will happen. It is important to bear in mind that any increase in clingy behaviour, and/or protesting at being left, are normal attachment behaviours of this age. Reassure your baby by ensuring that she is not left to the point of becoming distressed if possible. Keep following a predictable bedtime routine or ritual each night at sleep time. This helps your baby prepare for sleep. A regular bedtime is becoming increasingly important for the establishment of a routine. Ensure that predictable patterns of behaviour occur consistently – for example feeding your baby when they wake, then playing and settling to sleep without another feed will reduce the likelihood of feeding to sleep becoming a problem. Consider using a night-light and introducing some comforting objects (see p. 121) to support self-soothing at night.

Ten to Twelve Months

Development

Thinking/feeling

The parts of the brain that are responsible for directing behaviour, planning and emotional regulation continue the developmental surge that started in the previous age section. This means that:

+ Self-control and self-regulation have improved a little more, though there is still obviously a long way to go. (There is another surge in the development of these skills in toddlerhood.)
+ Your baby is starting to become more aware of his feelings, and perhaps even those of others. Babies at this age have been observed to become agitated and disturbed when they see their mothers distressed, the first signs of what will develop into empathy.[28]
+ There is a surge in the development of your baby's memory capacity and ability to recall information.
+ With limit setting comes the likely onset of *shame* in your baby, an important human emotion that keeps us behaving in socially acceptable ways. Shame feels pretty horrible though so your baby may need your help recovering after he has been told 'no' or shown a disapproving look. (Helping a baby recover means getting over the event yourself and showing that you are still available and caring even when your baby has done the 'wrong' thing.)

Behaviour and motor skills

+ Many babies are on the move now, in one form or another (crawling, rolling, shuffling or even walking!).
+ Your baby still has considerable trouble controlling himself, and needs limits to be set for him (around safety) by his caregivers. Babies may become upset

Ten to Twelve Months

or frustrated at being told 'no', or having their plans thwarted, and may need another's help to calm down after such an upset.
+ Your baby can understand more words and phrases spoken regularly near, and to them (such as 'mum', 'dad', 'milk', 'what's that?', 'hello', 'goodbye', 'goodnight' and 'no').
+ Babies may be able to follow through with simple instructions, such as 'give Mummy the cup, please'.
+ Your baby's increased understanding of the world around her helps explain why she may be having trouble getting off to sleep, because now:
  – she doesn't want to be alone
  – she is aware that things are happening around her and she doesn't want to miss out
  – she wants to practise new skills such as standing, crawling or walking.

Sleep

+ Your baby may have difficulty falling asleep if she isn't tired enough, particularly if she has not had the opportunity for physical activity.
+ Babies have fully adapted to the light/dark cycle meaning your baby should be sleeping longer periods at night compared to during the day.[23]
+ Many babies are now having two day sleeps. In the next couple of months, some babies will be ready to move to just one day sleep.
+ Total sleep time averages 12–16 hours per 24-hour day.[23]
+ REM sleep still makes up about 30 per cent of sleep time.[23] This means babies still have a lot of light active sleep and may still rouse from sleep often and easily, particularly in the early hours of the morning.
+ Night-time waking may still occur around this age, as there is a continued surge in attachment needs, brain development and physical activity.

What to expect

+ Your baby can now remember and even predict behaviour patterns. Depending on their temperament, some babies may become unsettled if something changes in their daily routine.
+ You may even notice that your baby is becoming even clingier and more demanding of your attention at this age. Attachment behaviours such as crying and clinging continue to be instinctual rather than intentional. This means that your baby is driven to want to stay near to you and isn't intentionally clinging to annoy you! Researchers think that this surge in attachment behaviours is because babies have now often developed the physical means to move around (and potentially away from their caregivers who keep them safe) so they need to *want* to stay near.[27,28] Because of all this, some babies may object to being left alone in their bed at this age. However, *you* know they are safe, so can help them to learn this too, by reassuring them that they are all right in their bed, and having the expectation that they can, and will go to sleep in their own bed. Over time, through repeated experience, the baby will come to learn this too. Objects or behaviours that support self-soothing are important at this age, and babies may become very attached to these (such as a comfort toy, lullaby toy, dummies). Thankfully, many babies learn to find and put in their own dummies at this age. You can help by leaving several dummies in their bed for them to find during sleep if you like (see p. 12 on dummies). A night-light may help at this age.
+ This is a 'practising' age, both physically and emotionally, for your baby. He needs support to practise new physical skills as well as emotional ones. It is important for him to have opportunities to practise experiencing different emotions such as excitement, happiness, frustration, and even shame and disappointment. The key is for you to allow these experiences, but help your baby to manage these new and sometimes powerful emotions so he is not overwhelmed. For example, you will now be needing to say 'no' to your baby at times and noticing his frustration and upset about this. These new emotions feel uncomfortable for your baby but

will pass in a minute or two with your help. Verbally acknowledging the emotion ('You are frustrated, I can see that') and physically (with a cuddle), while not making a big deal of it is helpful for your baby.

Parental challenges

+ Learning how to tell if your baby is expressing a genuine need, or if he is demanding something that he *wants*, but doesn't necessarily *need* (which may still be indulged of course, but does not have to be).
+ Clinginess and stranger anxiety may present a challenge for some parents. Understanding why your baby is clingy at this time may help, and also realising that this is a phase that will pass.

Table 16: A possible daily routine for a child at ten to 12 months.

TIME	ACTIVITY
7 am	Milk feed on waking (may be from breast, bottle or cup)
	Breakfast
	Playtime/awake time for 2 to 3 hours
9 am	Sleep for an hour or two
11 am–noon	Lunch
	Milk feed (may be from breast, bottle or cup)
	Playtime/awake time for 1 to 2 hours
2 pm	Sleep for an hour or two
4 pm	Milk feed and/or afternoon snack
	Playtime/awake time
6 pm	Dinner (solids)
	Bath or wash and ready for bed
	Milk feed
7 pm	Settle to sleep
10–11 pm	Rollover feed if you are doing one

Some babies may still be waking in the night for a feed. See p. 130 for tips on how to reduce this.

(Remember, this is an example of a routine only, and your routine must suit your circumstances. See p. 118 for tips on developing a routine.)

Ten to Twelve Months

Table 17: Baby sleep at a glance: ten to 12 months.

WHAT TO EXPECT	TIPS
This is an age for practice, both physical and emotional skills.	Introduce limit setting to a baby testing the wonders of cause and effect.
The development of the area of the brain responsible for self-control and emotional regulation is continuing. As is your baby's understanding of cause and effect.	Remember that increases in clingy behaviour, and/or protesting about being left are normal attachment behaviours of this age.
Understanding of language is improving.	Reassure your baby by ensuring that she is not left to the point of becoming distressed if possible. Now she understands more, talking to her can help reassure her.
Most babies will now be having 2 daytime naps at predictable times during the day.	
As your baby begins to move there can be an increase in attachment behaviours because he is pre-wired to stay close to you for his safety.	Consider using a night-light and introducing a comforting object (see p. 121 to support self-soothing at night).

Ten to Twelve Months

Case study

Limits about sleep at night

When my baby was about 11 months old the World Cup soccer — featuring Australia — was on telly in the middle of the night. My daughter usually slept pretty well, but around midnight one night she woke and called for me. I was awake watching the game (and didn't want to miss a minute of it!), so I decided I would get her up to hang out with me. We had a fun couple of hours, watching the game and being together, cheering and clapping (not loud enough to wake the rest of the house), and we both went to bed (after some milk for her) after 2 am.

About 1 am the next night I was fast asleep when she called to me from her room. When I went in to see what she wanted she was standing in her cot looking excitedly at me, obviously ready for another fun night watching the telly with Mum! I had to explain to her that it was sleep time, that I had been asleep, and there was no football on that night. Of course she cried and protested and called me a couple more times just to check I wasn't having fun without her, and then she settled back into her usual sleep pattern. I felt a bit guilty about giving her mixed messages about what happens in the middle of the night, but also happy to have spent time barracking with her. I wasn't prepared to let my guilt about mixed messages convince me I should get her up again, and I felt confident she could handle the usual limits I set around sleep.

Angela, mother of Harriet

The COTSS Method (Creating Opportunities To Self-Soothe) for ten to twelve months

The following steps show you how to give your baby the opportunity to use some self-soothing skills around sleep time.

1. Start slowing and calming your activity around your baby as sleep time approaches.
2. Check that your baby's needs have been take care of (clean nappy, fed, burped, etc.).
3. Take your baby to her sleep room.
4. Read a book together, sing a bedtime song.
5. Wrap her (if you are still using a wrap).
6. Give your baby her sleep aid (such as a dummy or cuddle toy).
7. Cuddle her in your arms, rock/sway/pat gently until she is relaxed. Relaxing lullaby music can be part of this ritual if you like.
8. Say, 'Ssh – it's sleep time,' or whatever else you like that sends the message that it is now sleep time (a short lullaby about sleep or closing eyes for example).
9. Put your baby down in the cot, activate her lullaby toy if she has one, and say goodnight. You can stay in the room sitting quietly in a chair or leave the room; it's up to you to decide what is best for you and your baby.
10. If your baby cries with distress go to her, look at her and say, 'It's time for sleep now,' or similar and then leave her to settle down.

If the crying escalates and she sounds as though she is getting distressed, repeat steps 7 to 10. You can even go back to step 4 if she gets cross and frustrated at being in your arms.

Ten to Twelve Months

Try not to leave your baby until she becomes *distressed,* as it will then take longer for her to calm down and be ready for sleep. If the crying is escalating (getting louder and more insistent) go and check what her needs are and take care of these, then leave her to the business of falling asleep. The trick is to avoid letting her get distressed, to go in before this time to take care of any needs, and allow her to then settle to sleep. Through your consistent behaviour at bedtime your baby will come to understand two things:

+ you are consistently there to take care of her needs
+ you have clear expectations of what happens around sleep time, and your behaviour is predictable.

Note that the Sensible Sleep Solution, which uses the COTSS techniques for calming and settling, does not recommend leaving a baby to cry in distress.

Conclusion

Poor sleep habits that start in the first year of your baby's life can continue throughout childhood and into adolescence, and may negatively affect development, not to mention be a nightmare for you, the exhausted parents. It is vital to get your baby off to the right start by guiding them towards healthy sleep habits.

We wrote this book to give you, as parents, the facts about infant sleep and development, up-to-date information based on evidence rather than myths, old wives' tales and opinions. Read it before you have your baby so by the time you arrive home with your newborn in your arms you have realistic expectations and some understanding of how you wish to proceed. Then dip into *The Sensible Sleep Solution* through that challenging first year for easy-to-access and understand information that will help you respond confidently to sleep issues in a way that suits your new family and the way you wish to raise your child.

Sarah and Angie

Glossary

Active sleep A light and active sleep, similar to the rapid eye movement (REM) sleep of adults.

Attachment As part of Attachment theory, the term attachment refers to the process by which a baby looks to another human to see, and respond to, their physical and emotional needs.

Attachment behaviours In babies, behaviours like crying, smiling, clinging, looking at Mum and Dad's faces and making those cute goo and gah noises. The behaviours ensure the primary caregiver (usually the mother) stays close by. Attachment behaviours are instinctual, pre-programmed and vital for survival because human babies need to have someone to take care of them.

Attachment theory A theory developed in the 1950s by psychoanalyst, John Bowlby, to explain and make sense of human relationships.

Body rocking Rhythmic rocking backwards and forwards, either while sitting or on all fours. Some babies may use this movement for self-soothing.

Calming techniques Strategies used by a caregiver to help a baby feel calm and relaxed.

Cerebellum The part of the brain responsible for motor control.

Cerebral cortex The cerebral cortex is the largest part of the brain, associated with 'higher brain' function such as reflective thought, emotional awareness, and personality formation. The cerebral cortex is quite undeveloped at birth, and is the slowest area of the brain to mature.

Colic A term used to explain 'excessive crying' (crying for at least three hours per day, three days a week for a period of longer than three weeks). Colic is not a diagnosis of a physical problem, although it is sometimes talked about as if it is.

Circadian rhythm The body's natural sleep/wake cycle that is determined by exposure to light and dark. Not established at birth.

Classical conditioning Classical conditioning is a basic form of learning in which an association is formed between two stimuli. An example of classical conditioning is repeatedly playing a piece of music while undergoing relaxation practice. Eventually the music alone will trigger a relaxed state.

Comfort toy A toy that brings comfort to a baby. See transitional object.

Conditioning See classical conditioning, operant conditioning and reinforcement.

Controlled crying Leaving a baby alone to cry for increasing lengths of time until they go to sleep. Sometimes called 'teaching a baby to sleep'.

Co-sleeping Sharing a sleeping space. In the context of infant sleep, it refers to a baby sleeping in the parental bed.

Create Opportunities to Self-Soothe (COTSS) Techniques to help a baby learn to fall sleep without help from others as part of the Sensible Sleep Solution.

Demand feeding Feeding babies when it appears they are hungry rather than waiting for a set (or scheduled) time. Usually refers to breastfeeding, but can also refer to bottle feeding.

Distress An emotion. Signs of distress in a baby include sobbing, sweating, screaming, a racing heart, a red face and a frantic look.

Dream feed See rollover feed.

Gastro-oesophageal reflux (GR or GOR) Refers to the occurrence of milk and food acids coming back up from the stomach into the oesophagus. GR occurs in infants due to an immature valve at the bottom of the oesophagus not sealing, leading to vomiting or 'spilling' and painful burning in the oesophagus.

Learning The acquisition of information as a result of experience.

Lullaby toy A toy that makes a soothing sound. May be used at bedtime to encourage the formation of a sleep association that will encourage self-soothing over time.

Non-rapid eye movement sleep (NREM) The part of sleep that develops from 'quiet sleep' and is characterised by quiet, restful and deep sleep.

Operant conditioning A form of learning in which a baby (or a child, dog, adult, or even rat) does a random action *by chance, not by intention* (such as waving their hands) which they then notice causes something to happen. What happens may be good or bad. If what happens is good (i.e. the mobile moves and is interesting to look at) the random behaviour is reinforced. When this 'chance event' (the hand waving) happens a number of times and the reward (the interesting thing to look at) happens at least some of the time, the baby eventually 'learns' to wave their hand to get something good. This form of learning probably occurs in the 'lower' part of the brain (the cerebellum) not in the 'higher' parts of the brain responsible for more conscious, intentional learning. This sort of learning is used in animal training.

Personality A person's characteristic emotional and social style due to a mix of both temperament and life experiences.

Rapid eye movement sleep (REM) A sleep stage that develops from 'active' sleep in infants. During REM, the eyes and brain are very active and dreams occur..

Recall memory The ability to call up an image in one's mind, without any prompt being necessary.

Reinforcement Used in relation to operant conditioning. Refers to an increase of a behaviour following a change in the environment. Reinforcement may be *positive* or *negative*. Positive reinforcement is an increase in a behaviour after a reward is given. Negative reinforcement is an increase in a behaviour after something unpleasant is removed.

Reflex An automatic physiological response to nerve stimulation that is not within conscious control.

Rollover feed (also called a 'dream feed') A milk feed (from breast or bottle) that is given last thing at night to a half-asleep baby in the hope they will sleep through the night.

Self-soothing The ability to calm oneself down after a disruption or upset.

Separation anxiety An emotional response to being separated from a loved one. A degree of separation anxiety is quite normal from about nine months of age.

Settling techniques Techniques aimed at helping a baby fall asleep.

SIDS (Sudden Infant Death Syndrome) The sudden and unexplained death of a baby while sleeping.

Sleep accident An accident causing injury or death that happens in a sleep space or while a baby is sleeping. Examples include suffocation, strangulation or entrapment.

Sleep aid A physical object (such as a dummy, a toy or a wrap) that assists in the process of falling asleep.

Sleep association A behaviour that comes, over time and regular use, to be associated with the process of falling asleep.

Swaddling See wrapping.

Transitional object An object that soothes and comforts a baby or child, and reminds the baby or child of the comfort that they get from their main caregiver. Examples of transitional objects are soft toys, blankets, or dolls.

Temperament A person's traits that they are born with, i.e. genetically determined.

White noise A meaningless and unobtrusive background noise such as a a fan or a radio off station that may help settle a very young baby.

Wrapping (also called swaddling) The practice of firmly securing a baby with a wrap (such as a sheet) to promote the sensation of security (such as experienced in the womb).

Resources

Parenting support
- A general practitioner or paediatrician
- An allied health worker (Child and Youth Health (CYH) nurse, early childhood nurse, or midwife)
- The parent helpline in your state or territory
  Australian Capital Territory (Parentline): 02 6287 3833
  New South Wales (Parent Line) 1300 1300 52
  Northern Territory (Parentline): 1300 301 300
  Queensland (Parentline): 1300 301 300
  South Australia (Parent Helpline): 1300 364 100
  Tasmania (Parenting Line): 1300 808 178
  Victoria (Parent Line): 132 289
  Western Australia (Parent Help): 08 6279 1200 or 1800 654 432
- Allied healthcare workers (e.g. psychologists). Ask your GP for information on allied health workers.

Useful websites

Sleep information and products
- www.sleepeducation.net.au
  (Australian Centre for Education in Sleep, run by Dr Sarah Blunden)
- www.sleep.org.au
  (Australasian Sleep Association)

Parenting advice
+ www.raisingchildren.com.au
+ www.abc.net.au
+ www.bubhub.com.au
+ www.parentingsa.gov.au
+ www.cyh.com

Other
+ www.beyondblue.org.au
   (Beyond Blue (Australia), the national depression initiative)

References

1. Owens J, France K, and Wiggs L. 'Behavioural and cognitive-behavioural interventions for sleep disorders in infants and children: A review', *Sleep Medicine Reviews*, 1999; 3: 281–302
2. Mindell J, Kuhn B, Lewin D, Meltzer L, and Sadeh A. 'Behavioral treatment of bedtime problems and night wakings in infants and young children', *Sleep*, 2006; 29: 1263–1276
3. Feber R and Kryger M, *Principles and Practice of Sleep Medicine in the Child*, 1995, Philadelphia: W.B. Saunders
4. Jenni O, Deboer T, and Achermann P. 'Development of the 24-hour rest-activity pattern in human infants', *Infant Behavioral Development*, 2005, 29: 143–452
5. Bandla H and Splaingard M, 'Sleep problems in children with common medical disorders', *Pediatric Clinics of North America*, 2004; 51: 203–207
6. Douglas A, *Sleep solutions for your baby, toddler and preschooler: the ultimate no-worry approach for each age and stage*, 2006, Ontario: John Wiley and Sons Canada Ltd
7. SIDS, Sids and kids: Reducing the risk of sudden infant death syndrome. 1997, National SIDS Council of Australia: Sydney
8. Pantley E, *The no-cry sleep solution: gentle ways to help your baby sleep through the night*, 2002, New York: McGraw Hill
9. Behnhamou I, 'Sleep disorders of early childhood: a review', *Mother Baby Clinics* 2000; 37: 190–196.
10. Omari T, 'Gastroesophageal reflux in infants: can a simple left side positioning strategy help this diagnostic and therapeutic conundrum?', *Minerva Pediatrica* 2008; 60: 193–200
11. Vandenplas Y, Belli D, Dupont C, Kneepkens C, and Heymans H, 'The relation between gastro-oesophageal reflux, sleeping position and sudden infant death and its impact on positional therapy', *European Journal of Pediatrics* 1997; 156: 104–106
12. Thomas A, Chess S, and Birch H, *Temperament and behavior disorders in children*, 1969, New York: New York University Press
13. Sears W, Sears M, *The baby book: everything you need to know about your baby – from birth to age two*, 1993, USA: Little, Brown and Company

14. Lieberman A, *The emotional life of the toddler*, 1993, New York: The Free Press
15. Karen R, *Becoming attached: first relationships and how they shape our capacity to love*, 1994, Oxford: Oxford University Press
16. Gerhardt S, *Why love matters: how affection shapes a baby's brain*, 2004, London: Routledge
17. Wang C and Ahmed P, 'Organisational learning: a critical review', *The Learning Organization: An International Journal*, 2003; 10: 8–17
18. Eliot L, *What's going on in there? How the brain and mind develop in the first five years of life*, 1999, London: Allen Lane, The Penguin Press
19. Hiscock H and Wake M, 'Randomised controlled trial of behavioural infant sleep intervention to improve infant sleep and maternal mood', *BMJ* 2002; 324: 1062–1065
20. Bowlby J, *A secure base: clinical applications of attachment theory*, 1988, London: Routledge
21. Lack L and Wright H, 'Treating chronobiological components of chronic insomnia', *Sleep Medicine*, 2007; 8: 637644
22. Fettling L, *Postnatal Depression: A practical guide for Australian families*, 2002, East Hawthorn, Vic: IP Communications
23. Mindell J, Owens J, and Carskadon M, 'Developmental features of sleep', *Child and Adolescent Psychiatric Clinics of North America* 1999; 8: 695–725
24. Feber R, *Solve your child's sleep problems*, 1998, New York: Fireside Publications
25. Biddulph S, *Raising babies: should under 3s go to the nursery?*, 2005, London Harper Thorsons
26. Sheldon S, 'Sleep in infants and children', in *Sleep: a comprehensive handbook*, T.L. Chong (ed.) 2006, John Wiley & Sons: New Jersey
27. Newton R, *The attachment connection: parenting a secure and confident child using the science of attachment theory*, 2008, Oakland: New Harbinger Publications
28. Rose L, *Learning to love: the developing relationships between mother, father and baby during the first year*, 2000, Camberwell, Victoria: ACER Press
29. Morris JA, 'The common bacterial toxins hypothesis of sudden infant death syndrome', *Immunology and Medical Microbiology*, 1999: 25 (1–2):11–17

Index

Active sleep 6, 84, 92, 99, 106, 116, 134, 156
Attachment 53–58, 124, 146, 156
Attachment parenting 56, 156
Baby blues 78
Bed sharing 19–20, 23
Bedding, for co-sleeping 23
Body rocking 127, 156
Bowlby, John 54
Brain development 58–62
Brain structure 58–60
Calming techniques, for baby 33
Calming techniques, for parents 37
Circadian rhythm 7, 64, 94, 99, 100, 156
Colic 39–40, 156
Comfort toy 11, 14, 157
Conditioning 62–66, 157
Controlled comforting (see controlled crying)
Controlled crying 157
    and sensible sleep solution 50–53, 65
    and learning 65–66
Coping with less sleep 72
Coping with a new baby 77
Cortisol 35, 98, 115
Co-sleeping 19–20, 23, 157

Creating Opportunities to Self-Soothe method (COTSS) 157
    the first three months 90–91
    three to ten months 111–112
    eight to twelve months 140–141
Crying baby (see also temperament) 34–39
    reasons 34, 35, 39, 53
    tips for handling 36, 38
    myths about 35
    ongoing crying 38–39
Day sleeps 101–102
Demand feeding 67–68
Depression, postnatal 78
Developing a routine, tips 118
Dieting 72–73
Distress
    baby 112, 157
    parent 78
Dream feed (see rollover feed)
Dummies 12
Ear infection 42
Exercise 73
Flat head 97
Fussy babies 30
Gastro-oesophageal reflux (GR or GOR) 42–45, 157
Head banging 127
High needs babies 30

Housework 75
Illness, baby 41–43
Learning 62–63, 157
    and controlled crying 65
Lullaby toy 11, 14, 157
Medical issues and night waking 42–43
Memory, baby 62
Moro reflex (see startle reflex)
Napping 101–102
Neuronal connections 60–62
Night waking and illness 42
Non-rapid eye movement sleep (NREM) 6, 84, 157
Pantley, Elizabeth 24
Personality 25, 158
Positional plagiocephaly (see flat head)
Postnatal depression 78–79
Postnatal psychosis 79
Quiet sleep 6–7, 84, 98, 106
Rapid eye movement sleep (REM) 6, 84, 158
Reducing night feeds, tips 130
Reflex 83, 158
Reflux, gastro-oesophageal 42–45, 157
Relationship/partnerships 76
Rest and relaxation 73–74
Rollover feed 110, 158
Room temperature 22
Routine development 7, 66–68, 87, 94, 101, 109, 118, 129
Routines and rituals 66–68
Safe sleeping guidelines 22–23
Secure attachment 55–57

Self-soothing 49–50, 85, 90, 107, 108, 111, 115, 126, 140, 158
Self-soothing toys 11
Sensible Sleep Solution 48
    and controlled crying 50–53, 65
    and learning 65
    and routines 67
    and self-soothing 49–49
Sensitive babies 30
Separation anxiety 124, 128, 136, 158
Setting limits 138
Settling techniques 33, 158
SIDS 21–25
Signs of distress, baby 112
Sleep associations 9, 12–15, 159
Sleep stages 6–7
Sleeping accidents 21
Soft toys 11, 14
Startle reflex 83
Swaddling 13, 15–17
Techniques to calm baby 33, 37
Temperament 25–33, 159
    and brain development 25
    and challenges 30–31
    effect on sleep 26–27
Temperature and illness 41
Temperature of room 23
Thumb sucking 13
Transitional objects 121
Unwell baby 41
Where will baby sleep 18–19
White noise 15, 37, 159
Wrapping 13, 15–17

Wakefield Press is an independent publishing and
distribution company based in Adelaide, South Australia.
We love good stories and publish beautiful books.
To see our full range of books, please visit our website at
www.wakefieldpress.com.au
where all titles are available for purchase.
To keep up with our latest releases, news and events,
subscribe to our monthly newsletter.

Find us!

Facebook: www.facebook.com/wakefield.press
Twitter: www.twitter.com/wakefieldpress
Instagram: www.instagram.com/wakefieldpress